CRYSTAL
for today's woman

Happy birthday
Aunty Sarah
lots of love

Iain & Rhiannon
xxxxx
1997

CRYSTAL DIVINATION
for today's woman

by

Cassandra Eason

foulsham
London • New York • Toronto • Sydney

foulsham

Bennetts Close, Cippenham, Berkshire SL1 5AP

ISBN 0-572-01998-X

Copyright © 1994 Cassandra Eason

Phototypeset in Great Britain by
Typesetting Solutions, Slough, Berkshire.
Printed in Great Britain by
Cox & Wyman Ltd, Reading, Berkshire.

CRYSTAL DIVINATION
for today's woman

CONTENTS

INTRODUCTION

When I was first told about the magical powers of crystals I was sceptical to say the least. I'd had my fill of crystals in childhood: Dad would be cursing wildly as he crouched over a little wooden box which took pride of place on the kitchen table. Wearing a heavy pair of head-phones and using a piece of wire called a cat's whisker, he tickled a tiny piece of crystal held in a miniature vice. With this nightly magic ritual he hoped (but never managed) to hear scraps of the BBC Light Programme. Mom was not impressed. Jostling for room to make the sandwiches for the next day's lunch she always managed to jog Dad just at the moment he'd made contact — or so he said.

'Who're you expecting to hear on that contraption anyway?' Mom would ask, 'the Archangel Gabriel? Why can't you keep pigeons like other men?'

In the end the crystal disappeared. I think it ended up in one of the sandwiches and we hired a television from Radio Rentals. Mom dosed us with senapods for a week, just in case. 'Crystals can be very dangerous in the wrong place,' she muttered darkly.

Thirty years on I was inclined to agree, when I was researching a book at a psychic fair in Birmingham and a lady with dangly earrings and rows of crystals, priced at slightly more thn the average satellite dish, proffered a stone that was 'calling me'.

'At that price,' I said, 'I think the name it's calling must be Rothschild.'

But then I moved to the Isle of Wight and found a piece of quartz on the beach — perhaps it was my Dad's bit recycled. Then the magic started flowing. It did not come from the crystal alone nor from me, but rather from the connection we made. Dad died years ago and my own kids turn their noses up at anything less than a Walkman with stereo headphones, but I realised Dad was right. You've got to keep trying in the hope that the magic will flow and we'll hear, not scraps of someone else's message, but our own inner voice and powers of inspiration.

As with other forms of female-friendly divination I have studied*, I found that the crystals did not predict that I was going to meet a tall dark handsome stranger who was going to sweep me off my feet or tell me who was going to win the 3.30 at Newmarket (more's the pity). But they did give me a fantastic insight into the situations which make up 95% of our everyday life.

I realised that by throwing different stones on a cloth, the answers would appear, not out of thin air but by that amazing mix of the power of the earth, sixth sense and a dose of Mom's common sense to stop me getting 'above myself'. For crystals keep our feet on the ground while linking us with the stars so that we can make gigantic imaginative leaps without bothering with the bits in between.

They offer not only a very effective form of divination for women but, through their energies, can put us in touch with our own natural powers of wisdom and intuition.

* See the Today's Woman series for other books by Cassandra Eason

WHAT ARE CRYSTALS?

Crystal means 'clear ice' from the Greek word *crystallos*. It was believed that in ancient times sacred water fell from the skies and was frozen by the Gods — Hercules dropped the Crystal of Truth from Mount Olympus and the pieces of white quartz crystal we find or buy today are said to be fragments of this. Other societies believe crystals to be frozen light — to the Aborigines, for example, this frozen light is said to contain the Great Spirit.

Quartz is the most common mineral on earth. Traditionally, the word 'crystal' refers to this clear white sparkling form of quartz, but today the term is used for any straight-edged and plane-faced mineral that occurs naturally, and includes rare and beautiful gemstone forms that we thought of as jewels in our childhood.

Throughout history, and in all lands, crystals and gems have been valued. One of the earliest written records of their healing properties is found in the Ancient Egyptian Papyrus Ebers, which is dated about 1,500 BC: amethyst, for example, was considered a remedy against snakebite. Later on it was also said to prevent drunkenness, and wealthier Romans would drink out of amethyst goblets. However, such practices haven't yet caught on in the Red Lion.

As for crystal divination, the Babylonians carved magical symbols on bloodstones in order to foretell the future. Runes too were often carved on stone in both the Nordic and Anglo-Saxon cultures (in *Runes for Today's Woman* in this series, I suggest you save a fortune by making your own set from the pebbles in the park).

A crystal takes many thousands of years to form. Quartz crystals are composed of a combination of silicon and oxygen. The discovery that quartz crystal vibrates regularly when an electrical charge is passed through it, has led to quartz crystals being used as a vital component in radios, televisions, computers and watches (which are more reliable than my father's old crystal set radio). Indeed, the invention by the Canadian W A Morrison of a quartz crystal clock that would keep time accurately to minute degrees of a second became vital for space travel.

We sense the powers of crystals intuitively without any training when we handle them. For crystals are an exciting and very tactile way of tuning in to our inner powers and determining our future paths. Few people are happy with crystal ball divination because conscious expectations get in the way. A far more effective method of divination is to throw small crystals or gems on to a cloth to get in tune with our unconcious wisdom and knowledge.

You don't have to go to the Kalahari desert to dig for your stones, nor pay out a fortune for star rubies or sapphires. You need only 20 small crystals or polished stones which should cost no more than 50-75p each — some you can pick up for free on beaches or even local urban hillsides. At this stage, how you find your stones, and whether or not they are genuine crystals, is less important than learning how to use them for divination to work out the choices before you.

In time, you may want to build up a set of divinatory crystals that are special to you. These may cost a little more, but can also be used for other crystal work, and I'll suggest further uses for your divinatory crystals in the last chapter. But if you're hard up right now don't feel you've got to wait for a change in fortune — raid your childhood button box for pearls and coloured glass buttons or even paint white pebbles with food colouring. My best yellow stone was picked up on our local beach where it had been dyed by years of exposure to the sea. Your inner magic will supplement the gaps in the crystal power until you have a set of crystals you feel happy using. Or simply buy one of each colour if you'd sooner start with the real thing — you'll need ten to begin with and I'll tell you the key stone in each case.

If you haven't got a natural source locally try a mineral shop. Most big towns have one, especially in tourist areas. Or visit a friendly, well-lit New Age shop where there are lots of dishes of crystals with the prices clearly displayed, so you can have a good rummage and find the right stone for you. Sometimes there will be a bargain box containing flawed stones — the odd line or crack won't matter as long as it's not likely to splinter the first time you throw the crystal. The gift shop in your local museum might sell them too — often you'll get a really nice gem for a quarter of the price you'd pay elsewhere — and you can be sure it's the genuine article.

Quartz hunting is a good excuse for a day trip to the seaside, and when you hold the dullest quartz to the light you'll be surprised by the transformation as the light shines through it. Clear and clouded quartz can be found on beaches, by lakes or rivers or on hillsides, especially if you have the tools with you to crack open a bigger bit of glinting rock. But don't expect to find the Koh-I-Noor Diamond at your local gravel pit — I'm always a bit sceptical when people tell me they've found a perfect, beautifully polished quartz in the road, though I'd really like to prove myself wrong.

I do believe crystals and stones are special and magical and can help us to heal our stresses and illnesses and uncover our destiny. But we shouldn't be inhibited by made-up rules about cleansing and rotating the crystals or following some complicated layout for throwing stones that gets in the way of the real issues. I have suggested stones that are easily available and reasonably priced but you may see others you prefer — my list is only a guide so go and look at what's on offer. You may come across stones I've never even heard of.

We can feel the power of our crystals whether they are surrounded by candles in a flower-filled room or jammed in our pocket on the 8.22 to Victoria.

After a year or so, you may find you've collected dozens and dozens of stones of all kinds. I've become a crystal addict, but none has cost me much more than £1. Sometimes I use the lot for divinatory readings, though I've noticed that however many or few crystals I choose from my bag the accuracy is amazing. I've known people pick out six dull brown stones and then are astonished when they see the full range of bright blue, green, pink, red and yellow gems they didn't pick. We mostly choose the stones that represent areas where we have a psychic hiccup, for if an area of life is going well you don't need a reading to tell you so. As I've said in other books, the *Today's Woman* magic operates on a road-sign system to warn you of potential hazards ahead — you may well be able to take that bend at 60 mph and still come up smiling.

For the vital ingredient of crystal divination lies ultimately not in the stones alone but in our own magical powers that can enable us to see round corners and avoid life's pitfalls. You don't need to cast diamonds on a golden cloth to galvanise your hidden energies into action. You and your 50p crystals are together the route to unleashing your own earth energies. So now let's gather our crystals, draw the cloth to throw them on and, in a short time, we can go on to make our fortunes.

THE CRYSTALS

You will eventually need two different stones of each colour listed: one richly coloured, shining or sparkling and the other of a more muted tone. If you can afford only one of each colour, you can still get very accurate readings. Just buy the one I have mentioned as the key stone in each case and use the overall colour meaning for divination. I've started with white stones and then black because these are at either end of the colour scale. White contains all other colours and so is a synthesis of them. Black absorbs all other colours and is a negation of them. We define crystal meanings in this system largely by colour. But crystal divination is more than a variation of colour magic. We also recognise the living energy of the crystal that can give us closer access to our hidden wisdom and so crystals are a very special sort of personal magic. For today, go out and find a stone somewhere — it need not be beautiful. Hold it and feel yourself close to the earth. Wash it, place it under your pillow and dream of the earth.

Day 1

Obtaining your crystals

Why do we need two stones of each colour, one dazzling and the other more subdued? All stones contain two complementary forces: a positive, masculine, physical, logical energy and a negative (in the sense of electrical charges), feminine, spiritual and intuitive power. This mirrors our own make-up. We all possess a masculine and feminine side, (Jung's animus and anima) and have both a creative, energising impetus and a nurturing, receptive side to our nature.

Crystals, like people, tend to have more of one type of energy than the other and so we can categorise stones as mainly either creative or receptive. This is useful in divination for showing us whether a 'go-for-it' or 'wait-and-see' approach is best at any particular time. Of course, white and black stones represent the extreme contrasts of these forces, so at one end of the scale you've got a white, sparkling quartz crystal that is positively bursting with pure oomph and at the other a dull, black stone that is absorbing everything like a sponge and hopefully storing what is of value.

It's very easy to work out the difference — you don't need a complicated crystal book nor will you have to memorise every name and type of stone. Indeed, though most people agree crystals have different kinds of energies, there is no real consensus as to how you define these, and two different books may give completely opposite categorisations. This is because there is no right and wrong, but the system I use gives you a simple rule of thumb to make your own decisions. It is based on looking at the crystals and, if in doubt, using your own intuition. And so long as one shade and intensity of any one colour represents the creative element, and the other the receptive (which you'll easily see when you buy two of each colour), you can't go wrong. Indeed, the beauty of crystals is that your energising stones will become more positive as you use them and the receptive stones gentler and more harmonious. Take yesterday's stone and put it in the garden or an open space. You have started building your future.

Day

3

Colour

In our readings, our first port of call will always be the overall colour of the crystal to find out its meaning in our lives. Then we can look at each crystal and decide whether it's a creative or receptive crystal which will cue us into the most effective strategy for dealing with our current situation. As I've said in previous books, the *Today's Woman* magic system steers you past the pitfalls and leaves you to enjoy the good bits. You know life's good, but it's useful to have a bit of magic to make the not-so-good bits better.

The hot colours of the red, yellow and orange stones will contain a lot of creative power, even in their gentler tones, so any crystal of these colours, even if it is the receptive aspect, will involve a degree of action. Green and blue, the mid-point colours of heart and mind, have a lot of overlap in their creative and receptive aspects. Violet and indigo (which I've combined for ease) have more of the gentler harmonising power of the receptive, even when they do sparkle or radiate light, and so tend to address spiritual rather than physical matters, and issues involving intuition. In addition, I've used pink, a link between the physical red and spiritual purple (the harmonising of the two extremes if we think of colour as radiating in a continuous circle). So, naturally enough, pink speaks of the reconciliation of opposites. Finally, I've used brown, the colour of the earth and common sense, a welcome balance to the others.

For, as I've said before, in practice it's rarely a case of 'all-or-nothing'. The 100% beefcake male or Ms Weeping Willow, sewing fine seams on her silken cushion, are stereotypes (though some still aspire to be like them), and while many women are dynamic, competitive and rely on left-brain functions in their working lives, most of us somehow still end up caring for the world and his family of lame ducks — and, admittedly, this is a vital part of a woman's nature. So, in crystals of each colour we have the mix of creative and receptive aspects in different proportions according to the needs of the moment.

Once you've applied your overall crystal meaning by colour you'll then see if the creative or receptive aspect is dominant.

If the stone you've picked is a dense, rich, vibrant shade of the colour or is especially sparkling and radiant it will have strong creative elements (though remember, it's rarely all or nothing). If the crystal is a more subtle shade with a softer sheen or is cloudy, milky or matt, it will probably be receptive. Of course, many modern stones you buy have been professionally tumbled and so shine more than their equivalents straight from the shore or earth, but even so there is still quite a difference in shade and the degree of shine between the creative and receptive stones. Add a second stone to yesterday's and make a positive plan for tomorrow.

Day
4

Let me give you a simple example in action. Loretta and Sue both pick a blue stone and straight away we know the key issue from the overall meaning of the colour. Divination is like a giant psychic mirror — it magnifies your psychic spots and blemishes. We usually pick out stones that reflect a problem issue or area — when things are hunky-dory they just flow on without needing any action and you'll probably be too busy whooping it up to have time for a reading. Blue is often regarded as the colour of the mind and concious knowledge and wisdom (the purples deal with the realms of the spirit and unconscious wisdom). So we know our blue stone is saying there's a matter Loretta and Sue need to look at consciously and with logical step-by-step thought, from A to B to C, as opposed to intuitive leaps. Being blue (and close to purple) the crystal links the issue with principles and

The crystals in action

ideals, so both women obviously feel strongly about rights and wrongs.

Now let's look at our two different blue stones. Loretta picks a dyed howzite, a peacock blue opaque stone that is often mistaken for a turquoise, except it's much cheaper to buy. The type of colour suggests it's a mainly creative stone because it's brilliant in hue, dense and rich in tone, and so represents the energetic, logical, active side of the mind. So Loretta needs to think incisively about her future course and be prepared to react in a logical and not emotional way. But it's blue and the overall meaning of blue involves altruistic thought. So, even when howzite or turquoise turns up, you're not talking about ruthless business deals, but the need to use logic to overcome prejudice or difficulty in an important moral issue, maybe where strong-arm tactics are threatening to win the day. And Loretta is facing a situation at work where the manager of the estate agency has suggested she should come in on a shady, but potentially lucrative, deal involving repossessed houses. This is very tempting since Loretta has financial problems and the scheme is within the law. But her blue stone reminds her not only of professional ethics but her own principles and that, logically, the consequences of being caught would ruin her future prospects. Before long the manager is found out by Head Office, when operating another dubious scheme.

Sue, on the other hand, throws the receptive blue stone, a transparent pale blue lace agate. She's still in the realms of the mind, but the pale colour adds fluidity and flexibility and softens the 'high horse' approach when it's a case of 'principles or die'.

Sue has been working for a degree as a mature student since the break-up of her marriage. She has always said that she would die rather than accept help from her wealthy parents, who thought she should stick with her faithless but well-connected husband. Now she needs to go to France for her final year of study and has used all her bank loan facilities. She throws the receptive stone and realises logically that it would be a tremendous waste to give up everything now. So she compromises and borrows the money from her parents, who have come to admire their daughter's independence.

Easy isn't it to spot the difference? When you collect your blue stones, put the two side by side (or indeed any of your contrasting two stones) and you will tell at once which is the creative stone and which is the receptive. I'm repeating this *ad nauseum* because this is the key to your future crystal work.

Sometimes both aspects will turn up in a reading, in which case you know, as with the blue stones, for example, that it's time to mull over the issue from all angles and maybe be prepared to compromise over the relatively unimportant bits, but stick at the others.

As you build up your own collection of stones over the months, you'll find you can easily categorise any new stones. But remember, as I said earlier, there are no rights and wrongs because, whatever crystal experts tell you, there is no definitive categorisation of stones for divination or magical purposes. At the end of the day, go along with your own feelings.

Day 5

Crystal shopping

First you need to buy or make a bag in which to keep your crystals — any kind of material is fine. Providing the stones aren't sharp-edged, they won't scratch or wear each other away unless you buy a really brittle one. Keep your stones in the bag as you learn their meanings. Once you've learned a few you can pick one out each day to discover your underlying mood. You might want to buy all the stones together in which case there's a full checklist at the back to save you scrabbling through the book. Or you might prefer to buy just a few at a time each week. The order of stones isn't sacred, but it makes learning easier. At the back of the book is a list of stones that I have found special which you might like to add to your basic collection. Remember to write the names of the stones you buy, and a brief description, either at the back of the book or in a special crystal notebook — you will find it's useful to record your readings. If you forget the name of a stone, there are many excellent and cheap pocket guides to geology.

You can then compare the pictures and descriptions of new stones. Note whether your stone is creative or receptive so that when you buy more stones later you won't get the same ones. Pick stones about the size of a 2p piece and flat enough not to roll off the cloth. It's useful to collect stones of a similar size and shape if you want to be sure your choice is totally unconscious, but there's no need to be rigid if you like a particular stone. Put another stone in your collection and close the door on an old grievance, or give up a futile pursuit.

Day
6

White

This is the colour of the first pair of stones you'll need. If you can afford only one of each colour to begin with, then buy a creative stone such as a clear crystal quartz because white is mainly a creative colour. White at its clearest and brightest is the ultimate in creativity. And whether the stone we throw is clear or cloudy, white tells us it's an energy issue when change is in the air and we need to take positive action. Maybe you need to make a new beginning, or find an extra surge of energy at work or in a relationship. Any white stone then is talking about you feeling all this energy within, all the paths you'd like to take and all the changes you'd like to make right now. White tells you of the enormous potential you've still got whatever age you happen to be — and you ignore this energy at your peril! If you do plod on regardless, you'll feel ratty and restless and become a pain to live with, so go for it and don't listen to the doubters and prophets of doom.

Creative white

Clear quartz is very cheap about 50 - 75p for a nice sparkling crystal, and obtainable almost anywhere. If you are in the money, you might buy a colourless zircon — the poor man's diamond, which has a diamond-like lustre. But watch out, to kiss a zircon is a traditional way of testing purity, so if you have been having a bit of illicit nooky I'm told your stone may turn black.

Creative white stones are the oomph bit and if you throw one, it shows you have the energy and ability to go for whatever is on offer, whether career-wise or in your personal life. But you're maybe hesitating and thinking, 'I couldn't' or 'It's not my style'. But this is the new you that has been bubbling away under the surface — just remember, it's never too late to make a fresh start. Don't stand around testing the water — you've got to leap first and look second. Each day add to your crystal store and today think of all your strengths and assets.

Day 7

Receptive white

For the cloudy stone you can either buy some milky quartz (again very cheap), some delicate, translucent snow quartz or simply find a white pebble, which is often limestone. Magnesite looks like creamy chewing gum, but if you want a translucent white stone, you can sometimes get white mother of pearl quite cheaply — or even free from the beach. My own favourite is the milky-white moonstone (moonstones come in blue, pale pink and creamy brown and can be recognised by their lovely soft iridiscent sheen). Why aren't they creative if they shine? Hold up your cloudy stone next to the harsher brightness of your clear quartz. It's like comparing moonlight (reflected light) and sunlight.

As I've said before, the price of a stone is no guide to its magic, and throwing the Crown Jewels wouldn't necessarily get better results. If you do come across a white stone of incredibly obscure origin, that appears in absolutely no geological book below PhD level, you can use it once you know what white means. Then work out whether it's dazzling or clear (creative) or has a softer (receptive) sheen etc. Whatever you take it to represent in your own system is what it will come to mean to you.

If you throw a receptive white stone, this indicates a slower, more gradual change, taking the first steps on a path that may not bear fruit for many years. It may be that you can't throw up your job or your current relationship or move house without hurting other people. Perhaps you're tied by financial constraints or dependent children. For every dramatic step, there are ten slower paths to the end of the street. So, in this case, you know in your heart that there must be a new beginning — after all, it is a white stone, but the changes will have to be more gradual and begin in a small way: sending for that brochure or starting home-study. It may even be that you need

Day

8

*Reading the
white stones*

to set aside part of your weekend so you get out of the house with your children, partner or friends, rather than frantically trying to catch up on the unfinished chores.

If you throw both white stones in a reading then obviously it's change time, but there's a danger that your all-or-nothing dynamic first step will fizzle out at the first obstacle — perhaps this has happened before and you've a trail of new starts that didn't get much beyond first base. Women especially find that the demands of the world tend to overtake their good intentions. They miss a class because the baby is sick or the boss throws a wobbler because they can't do overtime. So it's important to recognise that more permanent improvement will come about only by overcoming each obstacle placed in the way. After that brilliant first day of nothing but mineral water and black grapes, it's daunting to face the next 100 days of sensible low-fat eating. It is easier to cope with five days crash followed by stuffing cream buns like they're going out of fashion. So, take one day at a time and keep going, adding to your stone pile or circle as you acquire more crystals. Each day decide on a positive action or let go of something which is redundant in your life — perhaps a useless emotion or habit. See how many steps you have already made to releasing the magic within you.

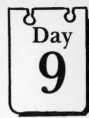

You'll eventually need two different kinds of black stone but, if you are starting with one, the key stone is the receptive one. Black is the ultimate receptive colour and absorbs or negates all other colours.

Black

At its most positive, black represents our ability to be open to others and to the world around us. These are the stones of waiting rather than rushing blindly into action and, most importantly, of endings rather than the new beginnings of the white crystals.

Black stones in divination do not mean someone is going to die, but they can represent a natural ending to a phase of life, whether the end of a time of living alone or the end of a relationship. Child-rearing involves many endings, not least the end of putting our own needs first. We watch children go to school, enter adolescence and when eventually they leave the nest, women end a role that has centred around mothering for so many years.

But equally, a decision to be childless or celibate closes certain doors. Sometimes these decisions are even imposed upon us. Or we may be retiring from a chosen career, or facing redundancy and trying desperately to hold on to what is familiar.

Women also empathise with the endings in the lives of partners which may involve radical change in their own lifestyles.

Such endings can be painful but there can be no new beginnings without them and it is only by embracing these change points, however they are caused, that we can move on to a whole new world of opportunities.

Creative black Choose a brilliant silvery black hematite, gleaming jet, or obsidian (if you hold this to the light you can see through it, as it is a type of natural glass). Even black onyx isn't prohibitively expensive if you buy a small piece. You can differentiate between this and an obsidian because you can't see through onyx. All these stones have a rich shine and a deep blackness and are very different from the softer colour of the receptive black stones.

The idea of creative black may sound a contradiction, but, as I said earlier, it's rarely all or nothing either with crystals or people. Creative black stones do hold a lot of energy, but because it's black it might indicate that you are wasting a lot of very vital personal power by either holding onto a situation or relationship that is redundant, or in suppressing negative and probably very justifiable feelings. Creative black is the shadow side we all have: the angers and resentments that do give us the impetus for change. Once worked through, they allow all that lovely white potential to be released.

Just find yourself a matt black pebble, perhaps a very dark piece of granite or flint. Or buy some very dark grey or black smoky quartz or banded agate that is predominantly black and dark grey. The agates will have a muted sheen if they have been tumbled or polished. But don't despise the black or very dark grey unpolished pebbles you find on the beach or in the park — mundane patches of life are as vital as those peak moments and this we can reflect in our crystal collection. If in doubt as to the difference between the creative and receptive stones put the two different kinds of black stones side by side, for example, gleaming silvery hematite and flint.

Receptive black

Receptive black suggests that you are feeling overwhelmed by the troubles and demands of the world and particularly of those nearest to you. This may be draining all your energies because you don't like saying no. You are a very nice person or you wouldn't have accepted all these impositions in the first place, but you probably end up with a permanent headache. Now is the time to draw limits and start saying no.

Day

11

Reading the black stones

If you get both black stones in a reading, then perhaps you think you don't have any right to feel angry or sad or to move on to the next stage in your life. Maybe you are stuck in the mothering role to your oversized baby birds or are propping up your parents' shaky marriage at the cost of your own personal freedom. Whatever burden you are carrying for others, now is the time to lay it down.

Your stone pile is growing. Once you have learned to read half a dozen crystals, you can start taking one every day from your bag. You may wish to record this and see what pattern emerges. Of course, the more crystals you learn the more representative your choice will be, but each crystal has its own message. You may like to carry the crystal you have selected around with you in your handbag or pocket, touching it when things get fraught as a reminder of your own inner strength and harmony.

Note the colour and whether it reveals a creative or receptive aspect. Practise putting your pairs of each colour side by side so you can see which is creative and which receptive. Remember the deep rich colour or sparkle of the creative stone is very different from the more muted or softer sheen of the receptive stone — the difference between the sun and the moon.

To illustrate the idea of a reading, let's eavesdrop on someone else's crystals over a three-day period.

Reading the stones

Paula's story

Paula is in her late twenties and has a rent-free flat in her parents' house. She is very successful at work but finds that every personal relationship founders as, although her parents have a rule never to interfere, she nevertheless senses their disapproval over her choice of partners. She feels inhibited about carrying on a sexual relationship though the accommodation is quite separate. Over three days and out of a full set of twenty crystals, Paula picks:

> Day 1 Black Receptive *A muted black-banded agate.*
> Day 2 Black Creative *A shiny piece of jet.*
> Day 3 White Creative *A piece of clear crystal quartz.*

Paula is clearly in a time warp. The black colour suggests that she has come to the end of a phase in her life and needs to move on. The two black stones together suggest a lot of negative feelings bubbling under the surface. These make Paula feel very guilty as she believes she has no right to feel resentful since she apparently has such a happy home life. And a rent-free flat is a definite incentive to remain her parents' little girl.

But at what price? The white creative crystal shows that nothing less than a major change will give Paula the freedom to develop personal and sexual relationships away from the protective, but stifling, parental nest. Had it been a cloudy white stone such as a moonstone or milky quartz, Paula would probably have found it easier to untie the bonds slowly. However the clear white stone tells Paula what she knows in her heart of hearts: it has got to be a complete change of living accommodation if she is to be free to grow up.

It will not be without pain, both financially and in the objections her parents may raise in her changing the status quo. But the alternative is the slow draining away of Paula's potential to form adult relationships.

Day 13

Red

If you are buying only one red, then choose a creative crystal as this is the key stone. Red is the colour of physical energy and action, putting into practice all those lovely white energies in a tangible way. It is the colour of courage and aggression. Men get very worried about aggressive women, branding them unfeminine. But sometimes we have to take a stand if the issue is an important one or if those we love are threatened.

When a red stone turns up in your readings, 10-1 a major injustice has been done to you or to someone you care for, and you feel angry. So red may be an assertion that enough is enough, a determination to change the unfair way things have been since the Dawn of Time when the mighty cave-dweller got the best bits of the meat and Mum was left tending the fire and washing up the stone saucepans as usual.

Forget rubies. If you want a sparkling *Creative red* stone try a deep red garnet — you can pick up a small piece of slightly flawed garnet for between £1 and £1.50. Red spinels are rarer and are often mistaken for rubies, but are equally dazzling — why not treat yourself? But if you want to keep the cost down, a carnelian (a form of chalcedony) is equally effective for divination. They can vary down through orange to salmon pink, but many come in a glowing, rich cherry red. Red jasper is also cheap and easily obtainable and has a vibrant opaque gleam. You can also get dark red rhodochrosite which can be glassy or pearly in hue, or red agate or blood agate which can resemble a carnelian, especially when highly polished, and is also a powerful creative stone.

Creative red suggests that you know in your heart that it is time to go into battle. This isn't easy because women often veer towards peace-making, and you realise that you will be making waves and ruffling more than a few feathers when you upset the status quo. But sometimes it's essential to take your courage in both hands and fight for what you know is important.

Day 14

If you enjoy searching around for your stones, this is one you can get for free. Look for a dark red pebble — you can usually find something, possibly sandstone or shale on hills or beaches, sometimes even in parks. If you prefer to shop around, you might find a piece of

Receptive red

red calcite that looks like a piece of ice or a lozenge. It is a bit brittle so choose a solid-looking chunk. Red fluorite is similar, though more like glass, or try some red banded agate which, though more opaque, often has muted reddish brown and pink colouring. On the whole, the banded agates, the true agate form in geological terms, tend to be more subdued in colour and so are usually receptive stones where the single richer coloured agates tend to be more creative.

Agates come in many single colours including black. Colouring tends to be a more reliable guide than stone type, so if in doubt use your eyes (backed up by your intuition) and you can't go wrong. You can easily see the difference when you put a garnet or a carnelian next to a piece of red fluorite or even the local sandstone pebble.

Receptive red suggests that you are turning your anger inwards and blaming yourself for the situation (others are only too eager to agree). This may leave you feeling depressed and perhaps eating too much, drinking too much or smoking too much. Stop biting the heads off cream buns and turn your anger on the true cause.

If you get both red stones in a reading then you're probably getting steamed up about unimportant issues, or arguing with yourself in the long hours of the night rather than tackling the real problem. Try to identify what's really bugging you — sometimes it can be painful to admit that it's not your friends being unfair to your new lover, or your daughter-in-law who's the villain of the piece, but rather someone nearer home. Once you've looked at the problem you may find it can be solved, at the very least you'll be able to sleep again or get through a day in the office without growling at the junior every five minutes.

This is the colour of independence, and often associated with the happiness and sense of uniqueness that gives us the confidence to assert who we are and what we believe, in spite of opposition from those around. It recognises our personal identity and says, 'Much as I love my friends and family, I am separate, and this is a good thing because only by loving myself can I love others.' It is the colour not of selfishness, but of awareness that our needs matter, that we can be happy in our own company and mustn't equate being alone with being lonely and rejected. So it's a very exciting stone to pick. If you are buying only one orange stone choose the creative orange as this is the key crystal for this colour.

We are spoilt for choice. My own favourite is amber, fossilised tree resin, usually about 50 million years old. It has a rich vibrant colour. Because it is so old it seems to emphasise the essential self which is always with us. Or you might pick a rich orange carnelian, vibrant opaque jasper or a sparkling orange citrine. It doesn't matter at all if you've got a red and orange carnelian in the same divination set because these colours are closely linked in the colour spectrum, and once you know the colour meaning you will see both carnelians and jaspers have creative energies in common in the sphere of action.

These crystals tend to appear if you start to notice that you no longer have the same goals as the crowd around you has, or at the time when you want to retire to Spain, your husband is sending for details of bungalows in Bognor. You can see how this desire for personal happiness, symbolised by the orange stone, could easily spill over into anger of the red stones. But the person or persons who are stifling you aren't being deliberately malicious. It may be that for years you've gone along with the opinions of others and they assume you will continue to have identical goals.

Now is the time to work out what would make you happy and how this can be achieved without anger or bitterness. (This leads us to the next colour yellow which represents communication) Of course, it may come as a shock to those around you to discover that you want to start college at an age when your friends are settling down to have families. But it's vital for your personal fulfilment to take over the reins of your life even if it's only deciding to give up dieting and accept that your shape is right for you.

Orange calcite is a soft ice-like stone that I especially like. Or you might choose an orange shade of smoky-quartz or a muted orange banded agate. There are some lovely beryl stones in a delicate, almost cloudy orange. But there are plenty of matt orange stones that you can get for nothing from beaches or hillsides (again usually sandstone or bits of quartzite that may have orange glints, depending on what other minerals are present).

Receptive orange

Receptive orange usually appears when we feel that our identity has disappeared. This often happens when women become mothers but it can occur in any situation — the young woman watching her boy-friend playing rugby week after week, then getting tea for his friends who gulp it down before going off to the pub to re-enact the triumphs of the day. Or an older woman can see her new-found freedom disappearing as she is expected to care for his newly-widowed mother. So start now to make time, however brief, for yourself. Begin to exercise your preferences — you may not even remember what they are. Many women, for example, cook to please others and have no idea what they really enjoy. It's a shock to find you don't really like meat when you've been serving up a Sunday roast for 15 years.

If you get both orange stones you may be living your life through other people: like the mother who pushes her children into higher education, perhaps to fulfil her own dreams, when the children might be happier going straight into some sort of practical career. Or you might be the sort of woman who is always the matchmaker but never gets romantically involved herself. Step out from the shadows and carve a place for yourself — the talents that serve others so well can be used to make your own life richer.

Whether your divination set consists entirely of gems, crystals or homely pebbles of the right colours, you will find that they have a magic of their own. If you get the chance, take them out into the moonlight, well away from the kids, your partner, even your best friend, and look at them and think about what they represent to you and your life and the way that you want to live.

Now you have learned eight stones, try picking one each morning out of your bag. As you learn to read more stones the choice will become more representative of your wider world. But all the stones address some aspect of ourselves. If you get the same crystal day after day, see how its meaning applies in your life and, as I said before, carry the stone in your bag or pocket if it is one you feel comfortable with. But first let's listen in on another reading where all the crystals were used, but those selected were stones we have come across.

Jane is in her late fifties and though she has a
good career it has been automatically assumed
that she will help out in any family emergency
as she has never married and has no permanent relationship. Now her mother has
become frail after a stroke, and Jane's
brothers and sister take it for granted that
Jane will give up her flat and job and move
home to take care of Mum. The family could
afford to pay for live-in help but they say it is
Jane's place since she has no commitments
and they don't want Mum to be left with
strangers. Jane draws:

Day 1 Creative red *A red carnelian.*
Day 2 Receptive orange *An orange beryl.*
Day 3 Receptive red *A banded red agate.*

Two red stones suggest that Jane is
angry about the situation — and quite
rightly. Creative red emphasises the injustice of Jane's being expected to drop
everything because she isn't married. Vic-
torian attitudes die hard.

The receptive red stone says that Jane
feels guilty that, deep down, she is the
selfish one. Because of this she isn't stat-
ing how she really feels which will ruffle a
few feathers when the rest of the family
realise they are involved in the problem
with Mum.

The two red stones together also indicate
that maybe there is more to the problem.
When I asked Jane she said that her
mother had always been very cold and
critical towards her, while her brothers, in
particular, could do no wrong, so it would
be especially hard for Jane to move
back home.

Finally the creative orange crystal tells Jane that her own needs have become submerged in the expectations of her family and that now is the time to assert that she does have needs of her own, that she exists as a person and not just the family first-aider. Of course, Jane will do her share of caring for Mum even if paid help is used, but it is vital that first of all Jane establishes her own separate identity in her own mind.

Making the cloth

This is very easy. All you need is a piece of fabric at least 12 inches square in a dark colour so you can see the crystals against it. I have drawn my circles and markings in gold permanent felt tip but you can use a plain black or any colour that shows up clearly. You will need to draw three circles.

THE ESSENTIAL YOU

THE INNER WORLD

THE EVERYDAY WORLD

THE REALM OF WAITING

Inner circle

Our inner circle talks of the core issues in our life, our fundamental beliefs, the real inner person without the window dressing. It is the essential you who, at the age of five, blacked the eye of the boy next door because he was hurting a kitten and who, at 80, will still be taking on developers who try to put motorways through conservation areas.

Middle circle

The middle circle is the circle of your inner world, your thoughts, hopes, fears, feelings and emotions. It is here that you argue with yourself, and others, in the middle of the night and maybe are too tired to tackle the real issue the next day. On the other hand you can formulate plans and dreams that can become reality, so it is also a very positive area for your crystals to fall in.

Outer circle

The outer circle is the area of your outer, everyday world. It is here that the action or hassles take place whether at an all-or-nothing level or at the level of mundane inconveniences.

Day 21

What if your crystals fall outside the circles, either on the table or the floor or in Aunty's lap as she dozes in the corner? I call this the Realm of Waiting, the area where, consciously or unconsciously, we hide the problems we can't face. Here we find the decisions that are too painful to deal with right now. So we need to be very kind to ourselves as we examine the

Outside the circles

crystals that fall outside the circles. For the skeletons we hide in the cupboard and the spectres we bolt our doors against don't go away. But if we can face them bit by bit then they can lose their power to haunt our sleep or pop out and spoil those times when all is going well.

You may find that the same crystals fall time and time again into this area. Perhaps this is because certain problems can't be solved without an unacceptable level of pain to those who depend on you. You may be burdened with an elderly relative who needs your devoted care for years and years, or a straying husband whose children are devoted to him and would be heartbroken if you kicked the brute out.

What other people see as intolerable we may have learned to live with as the lesser of two evils. A constant dull pain is bearable when a sudden vicious pain can be fatal, if not to yourself then to someone else you love.

So the stones may be saying that for now the business of living, paying the mortgage or coping with a family are taking all your time and energy. But don't fret about what you ought, in an ideal world to change. Most of us accept that life is less than perfect and concentrate on the areas where we can be happy. The crystals operate in the real world and one day those obstacles will come into the circles and you can tackle them. But for now leave them be.

Put the stones you have learned into your bag and pull out three without looking and throw them in the direction of the cloth. Whether you throw them one at a time or all three together is up to you. They may fall in a heap or may scatter in different directions. You can tell quite a lot from this, as the way the stones fall may reflect the way you are feeling: fractured and pulled in different directions or one thing piling on top of another. Or they may point you towards a particular area.

A cast of three

Then read the stones separately according to their colour and whether they are receptive or creative (if you're only using one of each colour just use the overall colour meaning). Don't forget, if two of the same colour do emerge than this issue is a key one. To make this seem easier we'll eavesdrop on a reading using the full range of 20 stones.

Lucille's story

Lucille's husband walked out on her three years ago when she was in her early 40s, leaving her with three children and a high mortgage. Now his new relationship has broken up and he has turned up at her door asking for a new start. The children are eager to have their dad back home, but Lucille has started to enjoy an independent life in spite of the difficulties. She throws:

> A creative black crystal *A pure black agate in the middle circle of her thoughts, hopes and fears.*
>
> A red creative crystal *A carnelian outside the circles in the area of waiting.*

*A white receptive crystal A moonstone in her
outer circle of everyday action.*

Immediately we can see how useful it is
to see the area where the crystals fall, as
this fine-tunes the meaning. A creative
black crystal suggests that Lucille is still
keeping the lid on a lot of unresolved hurt
and bitterness at the expense of her own
peace of mind. Her resentment is not only
at her husband's initial desertion, but also
at the fact that he thinks he can just come
back and pick up from where he left off.
So before making any decisions she needs
to share her thoughts and repressed
feelings with a sympathetic outsider, a
good friend or counsellor who will help
her to clear all those dark feelings that are
stopping her moving forward, whether
independently or with her former partner.

A red crystal continues this theme and
shows that there is real anger that Lucille
has suppressed because she is afraid of
the strength of her feelings. But she
obviously isn't (and shouldn't be) ready to
go forward until the past has been
resolved and her anger acknowledged.
Like many mothers in times of crisis,
Lucille has kept the lid on her negative
feelings for the sake of the children, but
sometimes this can give them a false picture of the situation and also maybe deny
their right to feel upset that Dad has
walked out.

The key is perhaps the white receptive
stone in the circle of her everyday world.
Any major change or new beginning,

whether it is with her husband or alone, can only be a very slow, step-by-step one, and it is important for everyone's sake that she isn't pressurised into instant decisions by her husband and the children. Three years is a long time and so it will take many months before Lucille can see which is the best way forward.

Day 23

Yellow

This is the colour of the sun and of communication. The clarity of the sun cuts through jargon and doublespeak, alerts us when the wool is being pulled over our eyes and banishes shadowy illusions. If you are buying only one crystal in this colour choose creative yellow as this is the key stone.

Creative yellow

These stones include sparkling yellow citrines, topaz or yellow zircons. You can also get a rich opaque yellow jasper or a golden yellow tiger's eye that has a beautiful lustre and rich striped markings. Some ambers too can be quite golden.

A creative yellow stone suggests that clear communication is needed to get things moving. This doesn't mean angry exchanges, but it is important to state your opinion in a way that allows for no misunderstandings or misinterpretation either of your views or the seriousness of your intentions. So it's not a time to throw a wobbler or sulk and hope people will ask you what is wrong. You've got to take the lead in negotiations, making sure that you aren't side-tracked.

*Receptive
yellow*

These stones include soft golden beryl, yellow calcite or yellow fluorite. I especially like a yellow rutilated quartz, the kind of crystal that is clouded inside with yellow or golden streaks — it is sometimes mistaken for a moonstone but is much yellower and doesn't have the moonstone's sheen. But on the shore, hills or parks you can find matt yellow pebbles, limestone, sandstone or shale for free. I have a very soft yellow quartz I found on my local beach on the Isle of Wight. It looks quite dull but when you hold it to the sun you can see the light. Crystals aren't only found in remote deserts or on exotic shores.

A receptive yellow crystal suggests that you may be confused in your own mind as to what it is you really want, or that you are overwhelmed by the seeming expertise of others. Equally you may not be hearing what is actually being said and this is causing unnecessary misunderstandings. Sometimes, especially in painful situations, we put up barriers and defeat ourselves in advance by anticipating the condemnation or superior knowledge of others. Leave yesterday's rejections behind and negotiate each situation afresh.

When you get both yellow stones in a reading, then it's time to work out the logistics, since there is something important to be negotiated. Spend a bit of time communicating with yourself. Clarify your objectives and work out how you can most effectively communicate them to others. Should you initiate a conversation, write a letter or make a phone call? The time and the place of such communications are equally crucial. It's no use trying to discuss the state of your marriage over breakfast when you're both rushing for trains. Nor is it appropriate to ask your boss for a rise when he's just been bawled out by the managing director, or has an important meeting to prepare for. It might sound trivial or unnecessary to mention, but time after time we do find ourselves blurting out something vital at quite the wrong moment because we've been concentrating on the what and not the where and how.

Reading the yellow stones

Don't feel you've got to stick to the types of stones I suggest. You may find a particularly lustrous version of a receptive stone or a softer shade of a creative one. This is especially true of the mid-colours like blue and green where the boundaries are blurred. So, at the last, let your eye be the guide. As I said, few people or crystals are all or nothing, and stones can come in many different shades and hues of the same colour, and some are far more lustrous than others. The divination system will work so long as you have a

Your stones

contrasting creative and receptive stone of each colour, as defined by you. The one you deem creative will appear in your readings when you need a bit of oomph and vice versa.

Even if you have only ten stones initially, there are five creative key stones and five receptive. So you can still tell in any reading whether you should adopt a 'go-for-it' or 'wait-and-see' approach by the predominance of either creative or receptive crystals.

Green

These crystals are the stones of our heart and so, when we choose them in a reading, it is our heart, not our head that is speaking. We are very aware of our own feelings about a situation and should for once be guided by them. For feelings as a guide to action are as important as thought, but too often we are taught to distrust them. Equally, we can sense the underlying emotions of others and can see beyond their words to the real meaning. At their best, green stones represent our ability to adapt our more rigid ideas to the real human situation. On the other hand, we shouldn't get wishy-washy and sentimental and end up offering a lot of sympathy, but not much pratical assistance. If you are only buying one green crystal, choose a receptive green stone because this is the key colour.

These include the brilliant emerald *Creative green* green opaque malachite, sometimes with black stripes or a pale green streak like a humbug. Or you can choose a deep green bloodstone, flecked with red, a form of chalcedony. Sometimes bloodstones are counted as red stones, but most have a predominantly green colour. The original bloodstone was said to have been made when the blood of Christ fell from the cross. Aventurines are similar in colour, a deep rich green with an opaque sheen (you can also get them in orange).

Of the sparkling clearer green stones, topaz has a green form as well as yellow. Green zircons are a good substitute for the more expensive emerald. Dark green spinels can also be transparent with a brilliant lustre, while the yellowy-green peridot is the dazzling sister of the more muted serpentine.

If you pick a creative green stone in a reading, then it indicates that, whatever sort of face you are showing to the outside world, you do feel strongly about a situation and should trust your own feelings rather than what others tell you or what seems logical. Don't let your usual sympathy for others and sensitivity to their feelings override what you know in your heart to be the real situation. Start at the heart of the matter and you won't go far wrong.

*Receptive
green*

These crystals include apple green chrysoprase, another form of chalcedony, soft jade which is found in many shades of green, greeny-blue and white-flecked amazonite, olive green serpentine, transparent green fluorite that may vary from light through to almost bottle green, but is usually soft in hue, and water ice green calcite. My own favourite is moss agate, though it is not strictly an agate; it is really colourless, but contains a profusion of tree-like growths of muted green minerals.

If you pick a receptive green stone in a reading then you shouldn't accept the situation at face value, but be aware of what people are feeling deep inside. This sensitivity and empathy for others, your greatest gift, will enable you to steer through a minefield of emotions, and resolve matters without diminishing the self-esteem of others. Sometimes when the red crystals appear and guns are blazing, a receptive green turns up, then the other person's underlying vulnerability comes onto your radar screen. So maybe it's time to try a sympathetic approach to your aggressor — swop the dragon and fair damsel or wicked hag and wronged maiden roles. The villain may be acting out of insecurity, not malice, in this instance. Use your empathic abilities well and you may find the bullying facade crumbling and a very unhappy little boy or girl sitting in the boss's chair saying, 'Nobody understands'. The receptive green crystal has extricated me from many a tight corner with authority.

If you get both green stones in a reading then maybe you're awash with emotion, there's not a dry eye or handkerchief in the place — neither is there a lot of practical action. So the crystals are asking you to think very deeply about what is genuine feeling and what is mere sentiment, what is real sorrow and what are crocodile tears.

Reading the green stones

The stones are also warning you not to allow yourself to be emotionally blackmailed by those who regard you as a soft touch. It's only your nice nature which has stopped you sitting down before now and drawing up a long list of those predators who know that a well-told hard luck story will have you reaching for your purse first, and worrying about how you are going to pay for your groceries later.

They are not necessarily nasty — they have just got used to depending on you. So you have to cancel your latest and greatest date, because your sister just can't manage the kids alone on Bank Holiday, while her husband is swanning off somewhere exotic on business. So you end up playing fond auntie and listening to her sorrows, instead of being wined and dined in style. And what happens when the swine of a hubby returns? He sweeps your sister of her feet with a bunch of red roses and you get left with a torn air ticket.

You are a natural giver, but all too often when *you* need a bit of support no one lifts a finger. Some of them just don't care, but in most cases they are so used to depending on you that they really cannot conceive of the tables being turned. So when your generous heart leaps and the two greens turn up, be sure you've got your own interests at heart, as well as the pond of lame ducks quacking at your door.

Day
29

A reading over three days

Are you picking the same crystal day after day? If so, what is it saying? If you are blocked, try finding its other half, the receptive or creative stone of the same colour, and carrying that around for a while or sleeping with it under your pillow. You may find that your perception becomes more balanced and you understand both sides of what may be a difficult situation.

Marcia's story
Marcia is about to leave school after taking her A levels and Mum has her matching suitcases ready for university. Dad is boasting about his daughter's brilliant future, but it's not what Marcia wants. She wants to train as a nurse and work in an East London teaching hospital where there are many social problems, but her parents won't hear of it. Marcia picks:

> Day 1 A creative green stone *A rich dark green aventurine.*
> Day 2 A creative yellow stone *A golden citrine.*
> Day 3 A receptive orange stone *A muted orange sandstone pebble from the beach.*

Two creative stones out of three suggest that Marcia should follow her dreams and not fulfil those of others. Perhaps Marcia's mum should try a crystal reading herself.

A creative green stone tells Marcia to follow what, in her heart, she knows will bring her happiness. Her feelings on the subject are stronger than she realises and for once she shouldn't let her parents guide her on the wrong path, however well-meaning their intentions.

Creative yellow is another 'go-for-it' stone. Here, it's saying that Marcia needs to communicate her feelings on the subject quite clearly, so that her parents realise that their little girl is serious. Hard though it is, she needs to argue her case logically — not throw a tantrum, cry or sulk, because that's what little girls do. Who knows? Mum may help to pack those brand new cases with nursing books once she gets used to the idea.

Receptive orange suggests Marcia still identifies herself as part of her parents and is so used to trying to please them, that she finds it hard to have her own ideas. When I talked to her about this, she said she had none of the usual teenage rows at home and this was the first major disagreement. So it is important for her to begin to establish a separate identity — even if Marcia ultimately goes along with her parents wishes — otherwise not only future career moves, but relationships too, may prove difficult. We met this situation in the first crystal reading when a grown-up baby bird was finding it difficult to have nooky under the parental roof.

As with many of the readings, the issue runs much deeper than the immediate question.

Day
30

Blue

This is the colour of the mind and conscious knowledge and wisdom. When blue stones appear in a reading, they indicate that this is a time to use logic and conventional thinking, rather than taking intuitive leaps. For this reason, blue stones are sometimes associated, quite wrongly, with men. In some primitive societies, only men would be allowed to wear rich blue stones, such as turquoise. But, at times, clear thought, unfettered by emotion is important for women to succeed in what is still a man's world. What is more, because blue is close to the more spiritual purple in the spectrum, principles and high ideals are usually central to whatever issue the stones highlight. If you are only buying one stone at first, choose the creative stone as this is the key one.

Creative blue

You can choose a dyed howzite, a sky-blue opaque turquoise, deep blue azurite, sometimes flecked with a paler blue, and the similar lapis lazuli or lazurite the traditional stone of the wisdom of the Gods that is flecked with gold. Or buy a falcon's eye a blue version of tiger's eye.

Laboradite, too, can sometimes have a brilliant bluey-green iridescence, though it also comes in more muted shades.

When you pick out a creative blue stone in a reading, there is a decision to be made involving more than material issues. Yet it's no good letting your heart rule your head. You've got to read the small print and calculate the cost, not only in financial terms, and weigh up the advantages of a short-term gain as opposed to possible long term benefits. There aren't any easy or sneaky cuts to riches or happiness; it's definitely a case of sticking to conventional wisdom and looking before you leap.

Day
31

Receptive
blue

These include pale blue, sheeny, lace agate or a clearer, dyed, pale blue quartz. Blue fluorite looks like a piece of smooth blue glass, while aquamarine, a form of beryl, varies between light and dark blue — the cheaper ones are pale and reflect the soft light of the sea in the early morning or at dusk. Celestite, with celestial blue tints, is another delicate receptive stone. My own favourite is a moonstone with a blue sheen.

Receptive blue still talks of the realms of the mind, but the pale colour indicates a need for fluidity and flexibility. It argues that you should soften the 'high horse' approach, even when you are sure that this is a time for sticking to your principles or dying.

You still can't let your feelings take over, but in this case it may be that you need to soften your logic with a little emotion, and to bend with the wind a little. You will still need to keep your wits about you, but it's better to compromise than stick out over every clause.

Day 32

Reading the blue stones

If both blue stones turn up in a reading, then you may be barking up the wrong tree and getting principled over an irrelevant issue while the real heart of the matter passes unnoticed. The crystals are suggesting that you should work out your bottom line: what is the absolute minimum that you must have? Where is your real sticking point? Then you should make detailed plans for achieving the main objective without losing your honour — or your shirt.

Air, the element often associated with the mind and logic, can vary between a hurricane and barely a breeze. And so with the two blue stones, you've got to know when to cut through the waffle and insist on accuracy and truth, and when to adopt the soft approach, letting the odd irrelevancy and bit of window dressing drift through without comment, because these points don't matter, and by disregarding them you can settle the bigger issues.

The double stones of whatever colour combine the creative and receptive aspects to make something more. To quote the often misquoted Gestalt theory: 'The whole is different from the sum of its parts'. So if, with the double blue stones

— as indeed with any double stones — you use the best of both aspects, you're onto a winner.

Plant a different herb or some seeds in your special place and keep adding a stone every day.

Violet, indigo or purple

These are the other side of the coin and deal with our unconscious wisdom, intuitions and inspirations. This elusive but vital part of our being links us with our spiritual and psychic self. It is the colour of our inner magical powers that can ease and illumine our everyday world if we just trust this hidden source. On a practical level, if you are in doubt, look at the question from a different angle and then leave it to your unconscious mind in dreams or waking visions to guide you.

If you are only buying one stone at first, pick the receptive purple stone as this is the key one.

Creative purple

Here we have opaque sodalite that comes in many shades of purple. Sodalite is very easy to obtain — deep indigo with white being the most common. Sugilite is more expensive, but comes in a beautiful bright purple, or you could choose a rich purple lapis lazuli. My own favourite is the iridescent peacock ore (bornite).

These stones suggest that you may be questioning the meaning and purpose of your life and are seeking fulfilment in a more spiritual or creative way. You shouldn't let people laugh or belittle any life changes you are making — trust yourself. The most successful woman can suddenly look at the sky or the trees outside the window and realise that there is another part of herself which needs fulfilling.

Day 34

Receptive purple

These include the soft, transparent amethyst crystals, which can vary from quite dark to almost colourless and are obtainable almost everywhere, purple fluorite and a lilac shade of transparent kunzite, sometimes called the woman's stone.

These are the stones of intuition, of seeing round corners and tell you this is a time to trust your hunches. The answer to your problems may involve going against everything you have been taught — how many times are we stopped from doing something by memories of being told from an early age, 'Nice girls don't do that' or, 'That's too expensive — don't waste your money' or, 'That's far too risky'?

But deep down inside you know that the course of action is right. Receptive purple is a confirmation that you are right to trust that inner knowledge, and it gives you the strength and confidence to face the everyday world with all its restrictions.

When you get both purple stones then it's time to make that leap into the dark and to trust your intuition to see you through. You know that there are no assurances at this point, but you are not alone — you have your inner star to guide you and hopefully your guardian angel to save you if you stumble.

Reading the
purple stones

It's time to combine your inner self with the face which you present to the everyday world. Being true to yourself is not just a New Age catch phrase which has no bearing on the real way you live. It is a concept as old as time itself and one which will still bear fruit today.

Because you have been working with stones of the spirit, it may be good for you to spend a little time down to earth in your garden. If the weather is nice, try to stay there for a while, absorbing the strength of the earth, and becoming aware of the free spirit that resides in us all, whether we are young and fresh or starting to fray a bit round the edges.

Now we've learned sixteen out of our twenty stones, we can begin to do full readings using the circles. You'll remember the circles were very simple:

Reading with
six crystals

> The centre circle stands for the essential you, your core beliefs and life and death issues.
> The middle circle is your inner world, your thoughts, hopes, fears and beliefs.

The outer circle is the outer everyday world where you cope on a practical and sometimes emotional level.

Take your six crystals out of the bag one at a time or as a set of three and throw the three on the cloth, or singly if you prefer. I find it easier to look at these three first and get the general drift of matters and then throw the next three to add to the picture. However, you may prefer to throw all six before you study the meanings, or even throw them in a handful rather than singly. There is no right or wrong way of doing this because any system is only a way of tapping into your unique inner magic. Ultimately it is formed, not by any book or guru, but by following your own intuitions. As I said for the cast of three, look at the way the stones fall. If they are all in a heap then you don't need divine inspiration to know they are related. Equally if they knock each other for six and scatter to the four winds, or at least to the corners of the cloth, then matters may be less than together in your personal and/or work spheres.

Day
37

A cast of six

Before we move on, let's look at someone else's reading. I was travelling on a train in the south of England when I gave this reading for Georgina, a successful businesswoman.

Georgina's story
Georgina told me how guilty she felt about having a bacon bap from the buffet. Why should she feel guilty? Because she had a new younger live-in partner, Gary, who, although he was out of work and relying on Georgina to

keep him, constantly undermined her with references to her weight — she had been about four stone overweight for most of her life — and accused her of being weak-willed every time another diet failed.

Recently at a party he and a very attractive colleague of hers flirted all evening. When Georgina tackled Gary afterwards he told her it was her own fault for being so fat. In a cast of six Georgina threw:

1 A receptive red stone *A piece of red calcite in her innermost circle of core issues and essential self.*

2 A creative orange stone *A piece of glowing amber in her middle circle of thoughts and feelings.*

3 A creative red stone *A carnelian in her outer area of waiting.*

4 A creative blue stone *A lapis lazuli in her innermost circle of core issues and essential self.*

5 A creative purple stone *A bright purple sugilite in her outer circle of the everday world.*

6 A receptive purple stone *A pale amethyst also in the circle of her everyday world.*

All the circles are represented, so we can deduce that the key issue, apparently her weight problem, affects every aspect of her being. Or is this masking a power ploy by someone less successful who is eager to keep her in the down position? Four of the six stones are creative, so it's clearly a time for action on Georgina's part, and that doesn't necessaily mean yet another diet.

The receptive red stone in her innermost circle suggests that Georgina is feeling angry, but probably throughout her life has swallowed her anger (and a lot of calories) because she feels deep down she is to blame. Georgina perhaps needs to accept that, fat or thin, we have a right to expect fidelity from our partners. Presumably her young partner didn't find her weight a problem in the early days and now perhaps is using it as a way of making her feel inferior, maybe because he is less successful in the world of work.

The creative orange stone in her middle circle of thoughts and feelings is all about Georgina's sense of identity. She doesn't need anyone else to define her as attractive and she is trying to fit into other people's ideas of perfection. Georgina has spent her life dieting and failing, perhaps because she is the shape that unconsciously she feels best at.

Her present partner is playing on this feeling of failure to excuse his own behaviour and it may be that, ultimately, Georgina finds she is happier without the put-downs in her life. On the other hand, once she asserts that she is happy with herself and has no intention of changing, then her partner may realise his ploy has failed and her salary is cushioning him from the cold world. This may be the aphrodisiac he needs to rekindle his earlier desire.

An additional clue is that both red stones have turned up. At the beginning of the reading I said that perhaps the weight issue wasn't the real problem. On the positive side, Georgina could perhaps help her boyfriend to acknowledge his own feelings of inadequacy and find ways in which they can support each other.

The creative blue stone in Georgina's innermost circle of core issues and essential self hints that it's not a time to let her heart or sentiments rule her head, or give way to emotional blackmail from her toy boy. While, in the short term, it's immensely reassuring and flattering to have a good-looking young man on her arm, in time she might be happier looking for a relationship based on mutual affection rather than physical charms and perhaps find a partner with a more mature attitude.

Both the creative purple stone and the receptive purple stone are in her outer circle of the everyday world. Two purple stones talk of making that leap in the dark and putting into action the change that you know won't necessarily bring fame or fortune, but is to do with following your inner star and doing what you really think is worthwhile with your life.

So what is Georgina's destiny? The ultimate diet that will succeed, a new relationship or a passionate reconciliation between two souls, whatever the difference in body size?

Georgina understood. The crystal reading had confirmed her growing realisation that she had spent much of her adult life searching for the ideal man and foolproof diet, and had compensated for failures in these fields by becoming successful in her job. However, what she really wanted to do was take a year off, live on her savings and try to make it as a serious novelist. So she decided to tell her boyfriend of her plans, explain she was what she was and would probably never be glamorous and take a chance he wouldn't leave when the money dried up. She got off at the next station so I never heard the end of her story, but I keep an eye out for her books.

You may find your own readings of six crystals just as illuminating so long as you trust your intuition and accept that what you think is the problem may only be a smokescreen. As I've said before, readings are like holding up a giant psychic mirror to your unconscious. When you see the spots you may recognise the cause and either decide to apply a remedy or let time take it's course. You know the right answer every time — you don't need to hire a clairvoyant, unless you want to take advantage of talking to someone who is very tuned in to other people. But, even then, only you can make the ultimate decisions.

Are your daily crystals changing, and do you get a progression of primarily creative or receptive stones? There are many clues if we listen to ourselves, and those friends and mentors, our bag of crystals.

Day 38

Pink

This isn't a primary colour on the spectrum, but it unites red, the colour with the longest wavelength, with violet, the colour with the shortest wavelength. Let's think of our crystal rainbow not purely as an arch in the sky but reflected in the sea as well, so the colours are in a circle not a straight line, just as women's lives run in cycles. Our outer lives often reflect our rich inner world and our crystals mirror the hidden aspects of us. If you are buying only one pink stone choose a receptive pink as this is the key crystal.

Pink represents the reconciliation of opposites or extremes and also of healing, and women are natural healers. It often appears when there's been a rift in the family, or in an important friendship, or even disharmony at work. Or your mind and body may feel fragmented and out of harmony and the crystals fly everywhere on the cloth when you throw them. But then a lovely pink stone appears right in the centre, or keeps popping up in daily readings and, being a woman, you know that whether there's internal or external strife, you'll be the one who has to heal the breach.

You might choose rich pink coral, which *Creative pink* is not actually a mineral nor a plant, but an organic gem made of calcium carbonate secreted by tiny invertebrates, or deep pink rhodonite that is sometimes streaked with black. Another common and not expensive pink creative stone is the rhodochrosite which has a colour range from bright to salmon pink and can often be banded with paler pink. The red version of this was one of the optional creative red stones. Sugilite also comes in bright pink (expensive, but worth buying) and you can occasionally get pink sodalite.

In a reading, these stones often appear when a conflict is external and directly involves you even if it wasn't your fault. Perhaps there's an awkward atmosphere at work or, following a disagreement, you've not heard from Mum, boyfriend or even a friend for a while. Somebody's got to break the deadlock, so maybe now's a good time to make overtures. I'm not suggesting you offer a grovelling apology, especially if you weren't to blame, but if the other person has got him or herself into a corner then your peace-offering can open the door to communication and reconciliation.

*Receptive
pink*

Here we have the very widely available, delicately transparent, rose quartz the translucent pink mother of pearl, or soft pink 'watermelon' tourmaline. Many tourmaline crystals are pink at one end and merge to green at the other, and are useful as an extra stone when you extend your collection, since they talk of reconciliation of matters of the heart. But initially it's better to choose plain pink to represent your receptive pink stone in your basic set of twenty. My own favourite is pink kunzite (the woman's stone) or a very pale pink calcite or pink fluorite. But you can get receptive pink stones such as pink and white flecked granite, or matt pink sandstone pebbles for free from the beach, hillside or even local recreation ground.

When you find a receptive pink crystal in a reading, the disharmony is usually within you and you are feeling tired and perhaps making a lot of mistakes without knowing why. It's time to slow down and rest whenever you can, eat easily-prepared nutritious meals and for now don't take on any unnecessary commitments. Avoid people and situations that cause you stress, though this isn't easy if, like me, the highest anxiety levels involve your nearest and sometimes dearest. Above all, be as kind to yourself as you would to your best friend or children, and nurture yourself till you feel restored. Often receptive pink stones will be thrown outside the circles into the area of waiting, for women are good at caring for others but often don't listen to their own needs.

If you get both pink stones in a reading then you may be standing in the middle of someone else's battle-ground. It's a great temptation for women to act as peacemakers between warring family members, friends or even colleagues at work. And women are expert at pouring oil on troubled waters and keeping people with very different interests together. But now your peace-making efforts are causing you to feel frazzled, while the combatants, whether it's your elderly mother and husband, or father and the teenagers, are getting off scot-free while you continue to act as the poor old UN peacekeeping force which gets shot at by both sides. So step out of the firing line for a while and at least let your own harmony be restored.

Day

40

Brown

This is the colour of the earth and can vary surprisingly in both vibrance and hue —look at a ploughed field in the sunlight and see how much richer that brown is than the sludge-like colour a toddler will make when let loose with a paint-box. And brown crystals, too, reflect this variance and richness and serve to remind us that crystals gain their energies from long years in the earth. So, when you choose a brown crystal it's telling you to go back to grass roots, touch home base and trust the evidence of your eyes, ears and other senses rather than rely on what you are told, read and see. The modern world bombards us with information, and because the media uses such effective and vivid techniques of presentation that can make even fiction seem fact, we tend to distrust the simpler knowledge that comes from our own observations. If in doubt, use your physical senses and especially your commonsense in situations that aren't clear-cut.

If you are buying only one brown stone initially choose the receptive version as this is the key stone.

Creative brown

These stones include the very widely available, rich, gleaming brown tiger's eye, the most common variety of this 'chatoyant' (reflecting a wavy band of light) form of quartz. There is also the lustrous brown chrysoberyl, rich brown amber, strongly-coloured rich brown or yellowy-brown jasper, and brown or tawny single-coloured agate. The more muted agate stones with several bands of fawny browns that merge into one another are useful as the receptive version of brown.

When you pick a creative brown stone in a reading then it's a nitty-gritty issue that's at the root of the problem. You'll need to take practical steps to resolve your problem and get things moving — it's not a 'back to the drawing board' approach or fine words that are needed. Commonsense and hard graft employed now may not move mountains, but at least can dig you a path.

These stones include petrified wood in various shades of brown that you can either buy polished or find on beaches where there were once prehistoric forests. These petrified wood pebbles are millions of years old and combine the richness of the earth with the power of the sea that flowed over the trees in later times.

Receptive brown

You can also buy various shades of smoky quartz or rutilated quartz, a clear quartz with golden-brown rutiles inside that stand for the hidden wisdom of the earth. You'll find lots of subtle brown stones in the cheaper baskets of polished pebbles in many gift or mineral shops, so choose any that appeal. My own favourites are the free stones: brown-stained limestones, perhaps containing fossils, or brown sandstone, or a browny flint. These homely matt pebbles represent the down-to-earth nature of the receptive brown stone.

When you pick a receptive brown stone you may be feeling overwhelmed by the sheer logistics of your life and exhausted with juggling the practical demands of work and home commitments. You're probably doing more than your share of the hard slog, whether it's cleaning the bathroom and kitchen of your shared flat because no-one else bothers, or trying to cope with meetings after nights awake with a teething baby, while your partner slumbers undisturbed in the spare room. So it's time for a little reorganisation on the practical front, even if it means that, for a while, you have to live in chaos while others get their acts together. Refuse to do more than your share (which being a woman is pretty large anyway) and if others won't pile in, then hire outside help and charge the easy-riders for the privilege.

If you get two brown stones in a reading, then commonsense isn't getting a hearing. You're used to absorbing the opinions of others and not arguing because there's enough disharmony without you adding your two penn'orth. Now you feel you're being taken for a ride but haven't got the confidence to assert your objections. Not surprisingly, the two brown stones often appear in the readings of mothers when they first start using crystal divination, but even women who are successful and assertive professionally sometimes take on the doormat or mouse role when it comes to personal relationships. If in doubt, go back to grass roots: how would you tell someone to react if they were in your position? Follow your own advice.

Reading the brown stones

Brown, as I have said, is not a colour to be despised. Your pebble collection may not gleam like your divination set, but it contains the power and stability of the earth. We need to touch home base regularly, whether by looking at our sleeping children, spending an evening gardening, or just by cleaning out a cupboard and perhaps rediscovering some old object which awakens memories of happy times. Life is lived on many levels and the higher we aspire, the more we need to know what we really value.

Let us look at Jade's reading over six days.

Jade's story

Jade is studying medicine and has recently moved into a new flat with three male medical students. Although they all work the same long hours Jade is expected to make coffee in the morning and cook for whoever is off-duty with her. She also cleans up the flat as she knows it would remain a complete shambles if she didn't do it. The others are very charming and do buy her the odd bunch of flowers and bottle of wine in gratitude. Now she has noticed that she is expected to do everyone else's washing as well as her own. The final straw came when one of the men, half-jokingly, complained he didn't have a clean shirt. Jade finds she is getting extremely ratty and tired and her flatmates have suggested she gets her hormones seen to. Jade picks over six days:

Day 1   A receptive brown stone *A smoky brown quartz.*

Day 2   A receptive pink stone *A pale rose quartz.*

Day 3   A receptive brown stone *Her smoky brown quartz again.*

Day 4   A receptive orange stone *A muted banded orange agate.*

Day 5   A receptive black stone *A piece of flint Jade found on the beach.*

Day 6   A receptive pink stone *Her rose quartz making a second appearance.*

The first thing to notice is that every one of Jade's stones is receptive, so she's absorbing an awful lot of other people's needs and demands. And clearly she's feeling so overwhelmed she's not likely to make a dynamic change overnight. It's not just traditionally reared older women who fall into the domestic trap. And today's modern male may still yearn for his home comforts.

Jade's receptive brown stone appears twice and confirms that it is the practical demands on her time that are largely responsible for her exhaustion and rattiness. So she will need to take one step at a time to withdraw from the nurturing role she has taken on. She works just as hard as the other students, so it is important she makes only her own coffee and cooks only her own meals until the others get the idea and maybe even suggest a rota — the male, when under pressure, is remarkably good at organising others.

Jade also picks her receptive pink stone twice which warns her that it really is time to cut down and restore her own physical and mental harmony by resting. Maybe, with all those doctors in the house, a few days in bed would do no harm, or a long trip home so that the guys discover that you don't need a PhD to clean the bath and that meals don't miraculously appear on the table like school dinners.

The receptive black stone confirms what is happening on the practical front, but suggests that Jade's dissatisfaction goes beyond the sheer physical slog. She feels responsible for the happiness of the home and this, as much as her flatmates' lack of consideration, keeps her in the Mother Courage role. When I asked about her childhood, she said her mother had been ill a lot, then her father used to get irritated and so she became used to trying to keep everyone happy. This has carried on into her adult life and so she believes that she is responsible for the well-being of others. Once she acknowledged this she felt much more able to be 'selfish'.

Her receptive orange stone developed this underlying theme. Because Jade had always lived for others, and even becoming a doctor was a continuation of her caring for humanity, she felt, albeit unconsciously, that she existed only in relation to other people. Therefore she naturally took on the running of the flat because it gave her a role, and this belief was strengthened by the flowers and chocolates. Jade agreed with this and said, in fact, she always asked the others what they wanted for dinner if they were home. So it's not as simple as it first appeared, selfish males and selfless female — though the guys weren't slow to take advantage of the domestic bliss on tap.

As I said, crystals have a remarkable way of getting to the heart of the issue which may reveal a very different problem from the one we thought we were facing. Sometimes we are actually setting up the situation that is apparently trapping us.

Crystal divination is perhaps the most easily accessed form of crystal power, and over the months and years, long after you've stopped using this book, your crystal collection will grow and change to reflect your changing needs. Picking a crystal every morning (and making a note of it) can be a very effective way of homing into those nocturnal dreams and visions that are only half-remembered and focusing yourself on the coming day. And readings of three or six using your crystal cloth pinpoint the choices before you and bring to the surface the underlying issues, resentments and guilts that may be preventing you from moving forward.

And remember, if you're broke you can start crystal divination with buttons or glass beads. However, once you do use crystals you'll find that their energies amplify your own inner magic. They needn't be expensive; some can be bought for the price of a chocolate bar and not only last longer but are better for you — I said you'd magically lose weight when you let your inner magic shine through. Don't forget, you can read with any number of crystals, and may want to buy others in the same colour. So long as you add a receptive crystal for every creative one — even if it's of a different colour — you'll keep the balance.

You will see that the crystals you need just turn up on the cloth no matter how many there are in the bag. I've thrown six green crystals (out of my bag of 70 or 80) at a time when I needed to use my heart, not my head. On another occasion six pink crystals appeared when I'd thrown a massive wobbler and was sulking in my cave. When you do get 30 crystals or more, you may wish to start to do occasional readings with nine crystals which you read just as three threes. In the appendix I've made a few suggestions of different ways in which you can use your crystals to enrich your life and mentioned one or two different crystals you might like to buy for general use.

We have passed 43 days together and there should be 43 stones in your garden, window box or wherever you've decided to keep them. You have learned the divination system and now you have years ahead of you to practise and perfect it in the way that you wish, so that you move towards the goals which you have chosen.

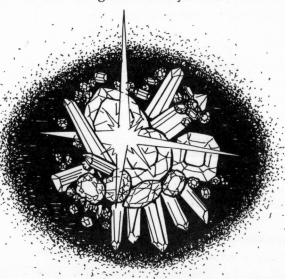

APPENDIX

The crystals that you use for divination can be used for other kinds of crystal work, for healing or for amplifying your own magical energies in a positive way. At the end of the book I've listed the crystals mentioned in each chapter so you've got a check-list, and I've also suggested a few more crystals you might like to buy and some you can find for free. You can get equally good results if you use your basic twenty stones, but with the price of a small crystal not much more than a chocolate bar you may find crystals a non-fattening, non-addictive way of reminding yourself what a very special person you are.

This section concentrates on crystal magic, for crystals can play a very positive part in both your everyday life and as a focus for your special inner world. There is nothing to learn — the 43 days gave you a basic divination system but whether expert or beginner, we all approach crystals in our own way and as we are talking about a relationship with our stones then there are no rights or wrongs.

Trusting your
Natural Crystal Knowledge
You don't need to be taught to handle or use your crystals any more than you need instruction on how to see a rainbow

or feel love. I've listed some ideas I find useful to trigger off your own work and I'd love to hear from readers who have discovered different approaches. You can contact me through the publisher and I'll not only reply but reflect your ideas in my next book on crystals.

Many books will tell you that you must follow certain rituals, or approach your crystals in special ways that have to be learned through expensive courses or in long manuals. But because we are all part of the earth as crystals are, we have natural affinities with them. We each of us carry deep down an instinctive knowledge of which crystal to wear or use when we are ill or need energy. And if your instincts run counter to what you read or are taught then trust yourself. Crystals are living but they only become magic when you use them as a focus for your own magical and earthly needs. I've heard scare stories of how putting a crystal to your 'third eye' can hurtle you into a world you can't control. But though crystals are to be respected and in time loved as dear friends, they aren't independent forces to take you over or hurt you if you choose the 'wrong one'.

Crystal magic is an area that tempts the 'insider' to exclude everyone else. If you are not careful you can find yourself asking a self-styled expert if you are holding your crystal the right way up and if you must move it from left to right or right to left. Crystals are very beautiful but, at the end of the day they are only tools, (albeit special ones for our own inner magic) so you can and should follow your inner voice as to what seems best.

Look at your crystals, handle them, sleep with them under your pillow, play with them as you played with the button box as a child. Crystals are fun, the fairy crown of childhood, the jewel box at the end of the rainbow — except your crystals won't fade at bedtime or the end of the film.

Our early fascination for jewels was a forerunner of later crystal work and I include a section on children and crystals for they perhaps understand crystals instinctively and we can learn much from watching a young child. So first let's go back and think about fairy wands.

A crystal wand
Remember those fairy tales where the godmother waved her magic wand and Cinderella got a golden coach, frilly frock and handsome prince in return for a couple of mice and a pumpkin?

Real-life wands are more practical because we don't want all our efforts disappearing at midnight. As for the handsome prince, you'd only end up massaging his ego and feeding his steed while he admired his reflection in his shiny armour. So seek the action for yourself. There are no free rides or lunches outside the story books, not unless we want to live on other people's terms.

For your wand buy a larger piece of quartz crystal, clear at one end and cloudy at the other. Either pointed at both ends or with the clear end (creative, positive) pointed and the clouded end (the receptive, negative as in electrical charge) rounded. Very Freudian! The crystal wand concentrates our positive and negative energies and kick-starts them into action. You needn't spend a fortune on your crystal wand or buy one of the ritual magic sort for sale through mail order or in the more witchey-poo New Age shops that are usually made of elaborately carved wood and supposedly contain a friendly tree spirit.

Shop around, and go for mineral shops or user-friendly New Age shops with the prices clearly displayed, rather than some dimly lit cavern with its crystals in glass cases or on blue velvet. The crystal wand need only be four or five inches long and should cost a few pounds at the most.

If you can't afford or don't want a wand, use your two white crystals from the divination set, the clear one for positive (same as creative) and a cloudy crystal quartz for the negative (receptive). Quartz is good for this distinction. So if you chose different white stones originally, you might want to buy a small piece of clear quartz and a second cloudy one instead of a wand but, the magic will work with any two creative and receptive white stones.

Your wand is very useful for concentrating your energies and getting new ideas off the ground. Remember white crystals stand for that new beginning and change points where you are bursting with energy.

Making Positive Magic

First decide what it is you want from your life starting from where you are right now and accepting any immovable restrictions. Make sure you really do want the change you are planning. This sounds contradictory — of course we want the handsome guy, exciting job and pots of money. Or do we? Often the reason we haven't got something is that when the chips are down, it's not as important as we thought and we'd sooner potter along on our own sniffing the flowers or settle for the nice lad next door. Which is fine if we are happy. For example, if you wanted to be rich more than anything else — and I'm not saying that would guarantee happiness — then you would concentrate your energies day and night to the exclusion of everything else.

Look at the number of people who have become millionaires even in times of high unemployment, starting with nothing. And that gives the clue to what real magic is all about. After the wand waving and chanting comes hard slog and more slog till you reach your goal, whatever it is, or decide you're happy to stop half-way up the mountain or the career ladder and concentrate your priorities elsewhere.

Of course there's always little Ms Perfect who apparently has it all with no effort whatsoever — though you'll usually find her daddy or granddaddy put in the blood, sweat and tears to provide the silver spoon in her mouth. And even then you'll usually find she spends three quarters of her leisure time exercising frantically and having tucks put in her vital parts and is never ever able to have the occasional pig-out like we lesser mortals.

Crystal magic for dynamic new beginnings.
Having decided what you want, find a quiet time and concentrate on your goal. Visualise yourself in that top job or exotic location with or without Mr Right — not two stone lighter and ten years younger but you as you are now — we're talking magic, not miracles! The early morning as the sun is coming up is a good time to work on new beginnings or in the evening at the New to Full Moon time (see *Moon Divination for Today's Woman*, published by Foulsham for more lunar magic).

If you wish, hold your wand in your left hand if you need to make an intuitive leap into the dark (the right side of the brain controls the intuitive and creative functions and the left side of the body). Use your right hand if you need to take logical, more conventional steps to fulfilment (the left side of the brain controls logical thought and planning and the right side of the body). If you forget this don't worry because your internal magic is used to filling in gaps.

Point the clear positive end of the crystal outwards and skywards because that's where we're aiming and keep fixing on that successful or happy you, a sort of souped-up version of the here and now model. If you are working indoors light a white candle (or yellow to strengthen your powers of communication) and ring it with all your creative crystals to concentrate your inner positive and creative energy on the desired change. Then blow out the candle and see all that lovely light at your disposal illuminating all the cobwebby bits of your psyche and propelling you to wherever it is you want to be.

Don't tell anyone what you are doing or let the kids or flatmates watch — not because you are dabbling with the occult, but because it's easy to feel daft and get discouraged. We aren't talking about harnessing powers out there but using our own inner magic and that's a very special personal process not even to be shared with our loved ones. And the magic does come from within you. You shouldn't ever try to call anything or anyone up, earthly or otherwise, to aid you. Whether you are getting in touch with psychic forces 'out there in the cosmos' or not, it is dangerous to rely on the gifts of others, whether known or unknown. And it's very tempting to make no effort yourself on the earthly plane if you're relying on spirits or higher powers to paddle your canoe. You and only you are in control.

So why use crystals in the first place if the powers are within us? Because of their natural energies. Ultrasonic waves have been picked up from stone circles such as the Rollright Stones in Oxfordshire. So your crystals can amplify that inner magic like a giant mirror reflecting sunlight. Indeed they become a part of your psyche as you use them.

I don't believe you need to keep your crystals untouched by others, or cleanse them if others use them or if you focus on them to get rid of your own grotty feelings. Others would disagree with me but I feel sure that physical rituals are of value only if we devise them spontaneously and if they are treated purely as symbols of our inner magic. The rituals I suggest are ones I find useful but, they are intended only to trigger off your own ideas and anyone who promises that if you follow their rites to the letter you will get instant wealth or happiness, really has spent too much time on higher planes and need to take a raincheck on common sense.

The magic bit is the easy part. Now you've got to keep the impetus going and make that change or new beginning happen: take that course, begin that new eating programme, or join the sports club right now, saggy bits and all. If it's love you want then it's no use mooning away the hours reading soppy romances. If you make a life for yourself and by yourself, then maybe you'll find that new love as a bonus. Funnily enough love is more likely to strike when you least need it — like getting a phone call you've been waiting for the minute you get in the bath.

Crystal magic for getting rid of old clutter

Again your magic wand or your two pieces of quartz crystal are useful for getting rid of unwanted luggage in your life. You can't use your quartz energies to get rid of people you don't like or to hex the boss or bad-tempered gran. Real magic doesn't work like that and if you start cursing people or trying to influence their actions as opposed to your own reactions to them, then you will at best end up with a headache.

What you can do is to concentrate your crystal energies towards changing your own attitude whether it's towards a critical person, a no-win situation or simply limitations imposed by old guilts or fears. If it's an inner problem hold the crystal in your left-hand for right-brain intervention and if it's a worldly outer issue use your right hand for the left-brain input. Hold the cloudy (negative end) outwards and point it towards the earth to let the bad vibes or feelings drain away. In any magic you should do something positive afterwards and since you are using crystal magic from the earth it's good to put a new plant in your garden or better still on a piece of waste ground as a way of saying thank you. This is much more effective than cleansing your crystal since you are redressing the balance in a creative way.

As you point your crystal downwards, visualise yourself walking away from the put-down or situation or shaking yourself like a wet dog and feeling lighter, free and at peace with yourself. Conventional magic often sees the object of your problem walking away in such spells but we can't and shouldn't try to influence others. But we can be responsible for our own destiny and so we can leave yesterday's luggage behind.

If you wish you can engrave the name of your guilt or dislike (not the person) on a stone and cast it into the sea or a pond. If you decide to bury it, plant something on top if only a packet of seeds, so good will come out of negative feelings and the flowers remind you when they grow of how far you've moved on. Sunset or the waning to dark of the moon are good times for banishing the redundant or unwanted.

If you are working indoors, ring a pink or purple (concilatory colours) candle with your receptive stones while you let go of the old hurts and as you blow out the candle let the light go to the person or situation that has galled you (after all you are in a mood to be generous).

Now comes the hard part — being positive in the following days. Above all, whenever you get rid of something, however unwanted, you've got to replace it or there's a vacuum in your life for the old regrets to sneak back. So conciously take up a new activity or go to a place you've always wanted to visit and keep moving forwards.

Sweet dreams

I've already suggested carrying the crystal you pick out from your bag each day around with you. But you may also find it helpful to do a bit of dream preparation for the day ahead if it's an important or tricky one. Each evening when you know you've got a particular issue to face the next day, take the two crystals of the relevant colour and sleep with them under your pillow (see check list at the end for a quick reminder of overall meanings). Your unconscious will be bevearing away all night and you may even find the answer comes in your dreams.If your problems are keeping you awake night after night then use your pink receptive stone to soothe you to sleep and send you sweet dreams (more of this in the crystal healing section.)

You may dream of ancient stone places, circles, barrows or standing stones — remember our stone piles in the garden we made during the 43 days. Or you may find yourself close to the shore or river bank or even on a hillside where there are many pebbles and stones. Whether this is dream or something more (see section on asral travel) your crystal dreams can offer the key to your waking world. You may meet either familiar people or those from long past and as you talk you'll feel comforted and discover that you aren't as alone as you thought.

If there's a choice to be made you may see two pathways, Sometimes they are identical but one may look stony, narrow and dark or uphill. Don't always opt for the easy path — around the corner may be unexpected open spaces — and from the top of the hill you may see the apparently easy path has petered out. Use your crystal as a guide — it's invariably there in your dream.

Crystal dreams can be very vivid and if you write them down they may offer insights into your present dilemmas or even issues or relationships you'd thought were clear-cut.

If you have a bad drem, you have only to feel for your crystal wand and it will protect you with its white light. You can then change your dream to the ending you want. Practise doing this with day-dreams until you can control your sleeping as well as waking world. When you have to live out those choices in the real world you aren't alone. You can feel your crystal in your pocket reminding you of your dreams and how you slew those dragons (or at least the one in the office) and went on to make a few of those dreams come true.

Crystal dreams are a rehearsal for reality and if you feel scared or depressed remember a happy dream and know that your crystal can help you to bridge the unconscious and conscious world and use your full powers to find happiness and confidence in the here and now.

Astral crystals

We do not know whether we actually visit other realms in our dreams and visions but such experiences can form an important part of our spiritual growth if we accept what they are telling us about our present world and dilemmas. I believe that whether we explore past lives or other planes psychically or psychologically, such wanderings are essentially a personal journey and we should not hand over our astral souls to anyone, even if he or she has a string of qualifications as long as the River Mersey.

Our stones can form a special doorway to these other worlds. You don't need an expensive crystal ball — indeed some people find them off-putting for divination as well as astral travel, since there is the underlying expectation you should see scenes in them like fish in a goldfish bowl. But the scenes we percieve using our crystals are those that come like daytime visions or dreams on our inner psychic screen.

You can get your astral stone for free or very cheaply. All you need is a stone with a hole made naturally in it — brown or grey pebbles from a riverbank or the beach that have in their colour the common sense and down to earth base we need when the spirit goes walkabout. Through this hole we can see those other worlds and dimensions often not in the physical sense but on a deeper level, in the mind's eye it is often called.

Or find or buy a stone containing a fossil. Ammonites, fossilised sea creatures are widely available. or use petrified wood. I found some on my local beach on the Isle of Wight that contained streaks of Fools' Gold (iron pyrites), a reminder to beware illusions. Jet, another fossilised wood, is also a powerful astral stone. All these through their long years in earth and water carry the wisdom of the ages they have existed through and so we can from their imprints access our own past wisdom.

Find a time to be quiet and alone with your astral stone. Why buy taped waterfalls when you can go for a walk? Even the centre of cities have hidden patches of natural beauty. Or use a corner of your garden. Mine is small but I've made myself a secret place, just a bench surrounded by fast growing hedging plants. Indoors is just as good so long as you are quiet and aren't worrying about your flatmates or kids bursting in. It's worthwhile planning this self time as carefully as you did some lovers' tryst in those golden teenage years when Romeo wore a leather jacket and wasn't ever going to turn into a carbon copy of your dad and spend Sundays at the DIY store.

Hold your astral stone in your left hand (to access the mysterious powers of the right brain) and don't try to relax or meditate, concentrate on the corner of the ceiling, conjure up a magic carpet or any of the other hackneyed tips for getting you off the ground. Let it happen — if your foot itches scratch it — and before you know it you'll glimpse a past scene or strange place. Just watch your inner movie screen — don't question or try to test the vision. Afterwards, make yourself a drink and take a few minutes seeing what your astral visit is saying about your life here and now.

If there was only a glimpse or two don't feel you got it wrong — there's all the time in the world and a good bit outside and each time you use your astral stone you'll fit another piece in the jigsaw.

You can use your astral stone when you visit an old house or museum. Keep it in your pocket or on a ribbon round your neck and you may find affinity with certain periods and places. Even if they aren't the exact place you maybe lived, there can be echoes that remind you of something you need to remember.

Take your crystal into the kitchen of a Stately Home or even to disused factories in an Industrial Museum. Or try restored cottages with straw rather than velvet on the floor — you may feel a sudden warmth or reminder, even maybe a chuckle or a shadow of a child or gran from that era. I felt very drawn to a needle maker's cottage in the West Midlands Industrial Museum and I sensed a sad, shabby old woman in the corner trying to attract my attention.

Being with my first husband who thought a liking for Bambi was a mental aberration, I didn't mention my experience. But years later I was researching my family history and I discovered my great-gran had been a needle maker until her health failed and she had been put in the workhouse.

Using your Crystal as a Pendulum

You may have a favourite pendant, your birthstone for example (see last section for list of birthstones), that you can use as a pendulum. For more details of divination with pendulums see *Pendulum Divination for Today's Woman*, (Foulsham, 1994). Or you might like to tie a cord, ribbon or chain round a long piece of clear crystal quartz. You can dowse for water, a lost object or to ascertain what you should do, using one response for yes, another for no and possibly a third if you are asking the wrong question (your crystal will guide you as to the meaning of the correct response).

Your crystal is a very sensitive detector of your inner knowledge. Though some people do see dowsing as a physical process, map dowsers are remarkably accurate in locating water or minerals merely from grid references. The crystal simply amplifies your own intuitions and gives them outer expression.

Many pendulums are made of quartz but a favourite amethyst or rose quartz pendant can bring a softness to the clarity of white quartz that is especially valuable in dowsing human problems.

If you can't decide between options write them on a piece of paper and hold your crystal over them — you don't even need a chain. I often use my crystal wand and pass it slowly from one option to the other. You'll find that it is drawn either as a yes movement or downwards like a magnet to the chosen answer and invariably this proves right.

If you don't feel well, use your crystal pendant or even a crystal without a cord to dowse over your body and find out the cause of the problem — you may be surprised at the result — (more of this in the healing section). Or write down possible causes and again, let your chosen crystal dowse the culprit — it may be dear old mum who is churning your innards from afar so don't forget to include a few people on your list if you suspect you're suffering from stress. Then write down possible solutions and again your crystal will guide you to the correct choice, probably the one you'd dismissed as out of the question.

Psychological and Psychic Protection

I've talked of using crystals to get rid of negative emotions. But sometimes we can sense that someone is hostile towards us or simply that the atmosphere in a place or our home is suddenly alien or unfriendly. Whether this is psychological or psychic we don't know. Certainly we shouldn't walk around in fear of being hexed if we've had a row with the next door neighbour. But if you feel worried or afraid — and often these fears outside are a reflection of some inner doubt — then you can use your favourite crystals to restore the harmony within, beyond or both, for they are closely connected.

Your crystal wand at your head and a receptive white stone at your feet, both receptives pointing outwards will absorb any negativity leaving you a safe haven to dream your dreams. And if you point the positive end of your wand towards you, then the lovely white energy will flow into you as you sleep, giving you creative dreams and filling you with energy for the next day. Or use your soft pink, purple, green and brown stones at the four corners. Visualise yourself in a lovely white crystal pyramid or a rose pink or purple of spirtuality and ask the angels of the crystals or the Light or Good or God or the Goddess or whoever you call protector to guard and guide you through the night.

If you sense a sudden wave of hostility either as a physical force from someone present or an unseen draining fear during the daytime, point your white creative crystal outwards to radiate your energy and see a huge silver shield come in front of you. The bad energies will bounce back, galvanised by your positive force. I once tried this with a gypsy who cursed me because I wouldn't buy her heather. I felt her hatred like a sheet of metal and I said, 'You can have that back' and it made a sound like wind through a bow as it reverberated away. As I walked on I noticed she'd fallen over. Coincidence?

You can hold a small crystal in your hand, pocket or bag and feel its energies protecting you if you know that you are going into unfriendly company. I often slip a rose quartz in my pocket if I know I'm lecturing to a potentially hostile audience or even doing a broadcast with a very aggressive interviewer.

I don't believe that afterwards you need to physically cleanse your crystals, though some people wash them under running water. But if you've used crystals as protection, you should thank them and perhaps light a white or purple candle and send light to those who tried to hurt you.

Do something positive to thank the Earth from which the crystals came, as I said when I talked of getting rid of negative thoughts, by planting some seeds, tidying litter or making extra sure your own packagings don't harm the environment. And if you can right an old quarrel or simply a coldness in a relationship, it does lessen the bad vibes flying round generally.

Crystal healing
Many books have been written on this subject but it is important not to let the complications of other people's theories

get in the way of the harmonising and healing power which your own relationship with your crystals can bring to your life. If you want to heal others I'd suggest you train through a proper association, such as the Federation of Spiritual Healers or the British Alliance of Healers Association. Equally if you want spiritual healing from an outside source apply to a registered association for reputable practitioners. Regrettably healing can attract frauds and profit makers.

But on a personal level crystals can be an effective way of restoring harmony to your mind and body that needs no formal training. Physical ills are increasingly being linked with stress and the discords of modern living. The problem with using conventional crystal healing guides is that they often recommend a specific colour or gem for a particular illness, e.g. blue stones to help with throat complaints or amethysts for headaches. Such ideas are based on a logical system since certain colours or gems are frequently associated with different chakras or energy centres of the body.

However, health problems are rarely that simple — for example stress or food allergies are often implicated in headaches and increasingly it's seen that a symptom in one part of the body can occur as a warning that we are generally 'out of sorts'.

So for healing I find it easier to use a creative/receptive distinction rather than trying to work out which colour goes with which ailment. Again the rule of thumb is based on what you see and feel. For example, if you're hot and headachey then a soothing green or blue receptive stone should help to right the balance. Equally, if you are feeling like a wet dish rag, a bit of creative red or orange crystal might get things going. If in doubt trust your instincts as to the right stone for you. There are no absolutes whatever anyone tells you or promises to teach you for a fat fee.

Lay all your stones on your cloth and see to which one you are drawn. We all have our favourites but, like a pregnant woman will instinctively crave foods her body needs to right a temporary nutritional deficiency, or an animal who knows which plants to eat when he is ill, we can access our inner wisdom to pick the stone or stones to right a particular ill. Then sit or lie quietly with your chosen crystal on the part where the pain or discomfort manifests itself most. Have a herbal bath — keep a selection hidden from the kids in colours and fragrances you like and pop your crystal in the water with you. I find for a headache a rose quartz or amethyst dipped in cold water and applied to my temple really helps.

But remember that pain is sometimes a warning that something is badly wrong. So use your discomfort as a warning sign to slow down and rest — the world really will survive without you for a day. If you have kids, leave them with videos and crisps for an afternoon or evening while you slump on the settee or huddle under your duvet. If the problem persists you should see a doctor. Crystals can and do galvanise our own immune systems but should be an additional tool not a substitute for the best in modern medecine and homeopathy.

Crystal calm

If you are feeling stressed and your muscles are screaming, lie down after your bath or sit on a big soft cushion or duvet and ring yourself with your receptive crystals. Light a very subtle incense and some soft pink or purple candles. Play some relaxing music and for now forget the overdraft, the teenager whose effort goes into his mad social whirl not his GCSEs or the carpings of your critical colleagues at work and let your thoughts roam free. Who knows where your crystals may take you? Anywhere is probably an improvement at the moment! Forget alcohol or chocolate bars that will only hype you up further and when you feel better eat something small that you really enjoy.

Crystal energy

If on the other hand you are flaked out, have a brightly coloured foamy bath and play some of the hits of your era (hijack the kids' personal stereo if you haven't got one but take care not to drop it in the foam). After your bath, ring yourself with all your creative crystals and light a red, orange or yellow candle and a more pungent incense. Forget the unmade beds, the unironed school uniforms and the letter you just have to write to Aunty. Plan what you would like to do (within possibility and the law) and than go and do it whether it's taking the kids for a moonlight hike, going for a bike ride, hiring a Beatles' video and twisting and shouting along, or repainting the living room. If you want to be alone, say so and let the world call back tomorrow.

Crystals and Fertility

Because many more women are beginning to have babies later in life, anxiety about fertility can be especially acute if you come off the pill and nothing happens. If you are over thirty-five — I'm an older mother myself — you'll want to check the physical side. If there is nothing physically wrong, it may be that for you, as for many women, anxiety is the greatest stumbling block to conception. Even if you are using artificial insemination or IVF, relaxation, positivity and a receptiveness can help to make conditions more favourable. Indeed one London hospital has introduced sessions of African dancing, mask making and drumming to overcome anxieties. Morris Dancing and May Revels prevented such problems in earlier times.

A favourite fertility crystal is the dragon's egg or thunder-egg that can be bought for a few pounds from a good New Age shop or mineral centre. Within the dull shell are crystalline formations (I especially like the purple or greeny subtle hues). Choose one with a top and bottom that fit together and leave a hollow inside. Dragon's eggs are best for this but if you can't get either use an ordinary empty egg shell dyed in a gentle receptive colour.

This represents the cosmic egg from which, according to so many legends, all life came. Inside the shell, place a tiny moonstone and put the egg on the window ledge at the end of your menstrual cycle. If you're lucky this may coincide with the new and waxing moon but it doesn't matter as it's your inner cycle that matters.

Open the egg and let any moonlight shine on the moonstone but close it during the day. When you are around ovulation — you may be using a thermometer or know from the mid-cycle pain some women feel and a restlessness that this is the right time — take your moonstone from the egg and place it under your pillow —the rest I'll leave to you.

Next morning put your moonstone back in the egg and keep it safe and protected, perhaps wrapped in a special shawl or scarf. Of course there are no guarantees but at least you are opening yourself to positive influences.

We know little of the relationship between the body and psyche. Crystals can act as a bridge between many realms and so often worries about fertility can, even without a physical cause reduce lovemaking to calendars, thermometers and rigid timings which can prevent the flow of spontaneous love and magic for that most wonderful act of love, creating a child.

Crystals and Pregnancy

In pregnancy a relationship begins with the unborn child almost from conception. Some women even have dreams and visions of their child before conception and these can prove remarkably accurate. (Many such incidents are recorded in my book *A Mother's Instincts*). Because pregnancy is such a magical time, even if you are being sick and get backache, your crystals can become an important bridge as you get to know your child within. You may find one special crystal becomes precious. If so, use it for it may be the crystal of your child even if it isn't the officially designated birthstone. Certainly this chosen stone may reflect characteristics you'll see in your baby when he or she is born:

White for a visionary.
Black for a nurturer.
Red for physical energy and courage.
Orange for a strong personality.
Yellow for a communicator.
Green for a loving heart.
Blue for idealism.
Purple for a psychic, spiritual child.
Pink for a peace-maker.
Brown for a practical, trustworthy offspring.

You may find, almost from conception, that you identify strongly with this one crystal, it may even be one which you have never really liked before. On the other hand, this awareness may grow with the foetus or you may find several crystals seem important — we all have many facets to our nature and your child may well be drawn in two or more directions.

You may wish to visualise your infant bathed in the colours of these crystals or in white, pink or purple. If you feel anxious or agitated connect with your child by gently circling his or her crystal over the womb. You may find one of the soothing colours useful if, like me, you have babies who seemed awake twenty four hours a day leaving my stomach feeling as if I'd been kicked by a mule.

Instinct will give you your own crystal rituals in pregnancy but, if you feel uncertain about your baby's personal crystal, picture him or her and pick one from your bag without looking. Unconscious wisdom can take over when anxieties block our inner vision. You might like to take your baby's crystal to the scan. If you have twins each will pick a different crystal. You might like to buy your baby a garment or item for the nursery in the chosen colour and perhaps make a mobile of tiny crystals to hang over the cot — most New Age shops sell them, sometimes with tiny bells to ring in the wind or when angels are close.

Crystals and Childbirth

For some women childbirth is a great glorious practically pain-free experience. For others it can be a thirty six hour continous contraction followed by a Caesarian. Neither reflects on your ability to relax, your fitness to be a mother or the later bonding experiences. But in either the very best or the very worse scenario, or most likely somewhere in between, your crystals are a link with all the other women throughout the ages who have touched another dimension as they give birth. You may want your baby's crystal with you and one or another may become precious as childbirth progresses as well as crystals of your own, perhaps red for energy, purple to rise above physical discomfort or green to help you go with the flow.

Afterwards, even in the most regimented impersonal hospital ward you can hold crystals above your baby as he or she focuses and in those early moments who knows what visions an infant beholds? If you get depressed or anxious when the world or hospital routine comes between you and your infant or your private space, you can hold your crystals and know that you are one with mothers everywhere and their love and wisdom are yours to tap.

You might like to retreat into your crystalline pavilion with the baby when the clatter of the ward becomes too great. And if you give birth at home, your crystals will be around you, greeting your child with light and colour. When you go home you may want to buy a crystal like your child's and place it in the ground with a new tree and watch the tree grow as your little one grows. Or if you live in a flat or apartment plant the crystal beneath a flower in a pot or window box and each year on your child's birthday scatter seeds on waste ground.

Crystals and Children

Children naturally love and understand crystals and treat them with respect — once they are old enough to realise you can't suck them. Even a baby loves to watch crystals dangling in the light and when children are three or four you can have largish crystals on your shelf and they will play treasures and all manner of imaginative games for hours. They seem to know instinctively which crystal to use if they are ill or in pain.

Night terrors can be diminished by a special crystal under a frightened child's pillow, especially rose quartz or one of the purple stones. Or your child may like to imagine himself or herself inside a crystal dome of their favourite colour, guarded by the angel of the crystal. You can see the angels in cloudy and rutilated quartz. As soon as your little one is old enough to understand, their personal crystal chosen before birth can become a very special treasure. But they will gain great pleasure from the simple stones of the garden or park, building with them, handling them — an unbreakable jar filled with water can keep them shining. And many a child's collection picked at random is an opening to the world of knowledge as they discover that stones are different not only in colour but in kind and realise that the magical and earthly world are only artificially divided.

Take your children to a museum (London's Natural History Museum is marvellous if you live near enough — there are many exhibits on minerals and the Earth's Core where children can handle objects and join in). Most towns have a geological section in the museum where there are examples not only of local crystals, but ones from far off places. Best of all are jewels found in Egyptian, Celtic or Roman remains or real treasure troves recovered from sunken ships or burial mounds where history and story combine.

Collecting Crystals

You might like to buy larger chunks of your favourite crystal to have around your house. Rough cut pieces of calcite, amethyst, quartz crystal and rose quartz shouldn't cost more than two or three pounds — again shop around. It's not the price that matters but whether you like the particular stone.

Over the years you can collect pieces of your favourites and use them to ring candles or your bed at times of stress or when you need a boost. It's not true the larger the pieces the more powerful the magic and some people always feel happier with small crystals they can slip in their pocket or bag.

But it is important not to forget the living stones we can't or shouldn't bring home. Standing stones and old burial mounds can be found throughout the world — in England, Stonehenge and Avebury are the best known but others such as the Rollrights in Oxfordshire, with their legend of the invading army turned to stone by the Hag of Rollright, are perhaps more magical because they are remote and less spoiled by tourism.

On the Isle of Wight (where I live) is the ancient Mottistone, high on the Downs, that formed a meeting place for the ancient tribes. But tempting though it is, don't bring a piece of the stone from an ancient site home — it won't rest and neither will you for it is a communal heritage and I'm not even sure we should charge to visit such monuments. It is important to prepare children for such visits by explaining the lives of the people who built the great circles and worshipped there and to find pictures of the stones in their full glory — that's where a prior visit to a museum can reap benefits.

But don't be surprised if they see a very different picture of their own — children are natural psychometrists, especially in the pre-school years and we can learn much by seeing history through their eyes rather than those of academics who may see the artefacts but not the emotions of these who used them.

Crystals as Presents

Crystals also make lovely presents for special friends and if you give a crystal away another one always turns up before long from an unexpected source — though as I said at the beginning you're unlikely to find the Koh-I-Noor diamond sitting in the middle of the A3 whatever the upmarket sources tell you.

Don't be afraid you are losing the protection of your crystals. A present in love or friendship enriches the giver. When I was in Los Angeles recently making a TV programme about my book *A Mother's Instincts,* I gave Hilary, one of the *Unsolved Mysteries* researchers with whom I had developed a friendship over the phone during the previous months, my crystal wand — to my own surprise as much as hers. Almost immediately I regretted it because the wand was very precious to me. The same night the worst earthquake for 20 years hit Los Angeles.

My own hotel, only ten miles from the Epicentre, was badly affected but I was unscathed. Hilary's home was quite close but though neighbouring properties were damaged, Hilary's little house was virtually untouched. The crystal wand remained on the window ledge where she had placed it throughout the quakes. Were we both lucky or something else?

I hadn't bought the wand in the first place. It had been unexpectedly sent to me by a dear friend Lilian who lived in the

Home Counties, because she'd suddenly thought of me as she was buying it for herself. I'd been hard-up at Christmas, a month before, and given a lot of my crystals as Christmas presents including a piece of quartz crystal I'd specially loved. I'd told no one but had been feeling very sad looking at the empty place and the next day the wand arrived.

Crystals for two

Though this book is in the *Today's Woman* series I know lots of men buy my books' and find them very helpful as they struggle to be gentle and caring in a world that pays lip service to the New Man but in practice still expects men to be left brain and not show emotion. Crystals are an excellent way of discovering undiscovered facets of you and a loved one or even a close friend. You'll find you pick different crystals with different people and this can vary according to circumstance. But in any relationship the first crystal you and a partner pick will be a key one in understanding the dynamics of your relationship.

Kerry and Jules were a thoroughly modern career couple in their thirties. Kerry worked in a bank as a Deputy Manager of a large branch while Jules was a social worker earning far less than Kerry. Jules did most of the practical housework. Kerry delved into her bag of twenty crystals and produced a receptive brown crystal, hardly the stone of a high flyer, more of a home-maker and nurturer. Jules in contrast picked out the creative white, energy, new ideas, ambition. Had the crystals got it wrong? Jules suggested that they'd got each other's crystals. Or deep down did they want to swap roles — time can change people's dreams. Kerry admitted she no longer enjoyed her high-flying career and had wanted to start a family and perhaps do some free-lance work from home. Jules had become interested in management and Social Services had offered to sponsor him to take a MA in Business Studies with a view to moving into administration. He felt he needed a change from case work and that caring had become more automatic. Neither Jules nor Kerry had said anything because it seemed to go against what they had set out to do.

So two crystals opened the way for each of them to talk about a very different future that wouldn't be easy but perhaps was the necessary progression in their lives and relationship.

With a friend, family member or partner, pick a crystal without looking. Return all the crystals to the bag as you may well pick the same stone, though often one partner picks a creative stone and the other a receptive. If you are unsure check the meanings at the back but don't be surprised if the crystals reveal totally unexpected facets. At the very least they are an opening gambit to discussion but can reveal hidden dreams and hopes that otherwise might have remained unspoken and unfulfilled.

Birth Crystals

There are many different versions of birth stone correspondences according to the culture and age from which the list emerges. And perhaps nowhere in the world of crystals is dogma more prevalent. No stone is lucky or unlucky whatever you may be told and because a stone is *your birthstone* according to a table in a book, you shouldn't feel you must buy it. What is important is not if you can afford for example a diamond, suggested sometimes for April, but if you feel an affinity to a particular crystal.

I've combined a very ancient list with some more modern versions — all of which differed — to suggest crystals that may cost you a fraction of a more precious gem, but are stones you can use in your crystal work — few would want to dowse with a ruby even if they could afford one. And the more precious stones can carry a fear of losing them — if I lose a cheaper crystal I'm sad but am glad someone else will find it who perhaps needs it.

If you don't feel attracted to the stones in my list or indeed any other birthstone list you may come across, then you should go to a New Age or mineral shop or indeed a shop that sells jewellery with semi-precious stones and see which stone you feel is special to you. All birth stone lists are drawn up by people, not deities and inevitably in time end up as a hotch-potch of traditions that were relevant to a particular era or belief system. A friend insists on wearing pearls because they are *her* birth stone according to the table she consults (she is a Cancer person) though she doesn't like pearls at all. In fact she'd sooner wear rose quartz that accords with her gentle, reconciliatory nature. Pre-birth stones too often correlate closer with a child's emerging personality than his or her listed birthstone.

If in doubt delve into your bag of crystals and ask: 'Which is my inner birth stone?' You may be surprised that it is a crystal you are often drawn to in jewellery displays or admire when worn by other people.

Suggested Crystals
Capricorn   (22 Dec-20 Jan)
Garnet for Fidelity.
Aquarius   (21 Jan-19 Feb)
Amethyst for Integrity.
Pisces   (20 Feb-20 Mar)
Rock Crystal for Vision.
Aries   (21 Mar-20 April)
Bloodstone for Determination.
Taurus   (21 April-21 May)
Amber for Tradition.
Gemini   (22 May-21 June)
Agate for Harmony.
Cancer   (22 June-22 July)
Moonstone for Unconscious Wisdom.
Leo   (23 July-23 Aug)
Carnelian for Courage.

Virgo   (24 Aug-23 Sept)
Jade for Self-Confidence.
Libra   (24 Sept-23 Oct)
Lapis Lazuli for Justice.
Scorpio   (24 Oct-22 Nov)
Aquamarine for Speaking True.
Sagittarius (23 Nov-21 Dec)
Citrine for Communication.

I'd love to hear from readers who do feel affinity with a particular stone and whether this is their *listed* birthstone. I'll report findings in my next book on the subject. Because as I've said before, any knowledge in these indefinable areas has to be personal and based on inutition and ultimately you are the best and only expert in your own magical properties.

Crystals in your Life

Trust yourself, whether in crystal divination, crystal magic or in life. There are no magic answers, no instant routes to the stars at the wave of a magic wand. But there is the enduring power of the earth flowing from your crystals that will amplify and magnify your inner magic. This book, like all those in the series for *Today's Woman,* is only a beginning to your own creative work and if it serves its purpose you will only look at it occasionally once you have learned the basic ideas. For no book, no fortune teller at psychic fair or the end of the pier or in an upmarket shop in Covent Garden or Fifth Avenue can be a substitute for your own instinctive abilities to guide and illuminate your path. Only you can and should shape your own destiny and follow your own star.

The most expensive gem or the humble pebble from your back yard are only as powerful as the psyche that joins with them — and that is your own special magic that makes you unique, lovely and loveable. Beauty and magic come from within. Love yourself and nurture yourself and you can do anything. So hold your favourite crystal that you have chosen and go forward in confidence that today is going to be better than yesterday because you will make it better, all the way to tomorrow.

SUMMARY

White

WHITE is the ultimate creative colour since it contains all others. If you are only buying one white stone pick a creative one as this is the key. White tells us it's an energy issue when change is in the air and you need to take positive action. There may be a new beginning you need to make or an extra surge of energy at work or in a relationship.

Creative White

Buy either:

Clear quartz *Cheap and obtainable almost anywhere.*

Colourless zircon *The poor man's diamond.*

Creative white stones are the oomph bit and when you throw one you have the energy and ability to go for whatever is on offer, whether career-wise or in your personal life. Don't stand around testing the water — you've got to leap and not look.

Receptive White

Buy one of these:

Milky quartz *Very cheap.*

Snow quartz *A delicate white.*

Magnesite *Like creamy chewing gum.*

White mother of pearl *Translucent.*
A white moonstone *Soft iridescent sheen.*
Or find a white pebble for free.
Receptive white says change will be slower, so take it a step at a time.

Black

BLACK is the ultimate receptive colour and absorbs all others. Therefore, if you are buying only one black stone choose a receptive one. Black represents the ending of a period in our lives, whether this is a natural change point or one forced on us by others. This will not be achieved without pain, but only then can we move on to the whole new world of opportunities that is waiting.

Creative Black

Buy one of these:
Hematite *Brilliant silvery black.*
Jet *Fossilised wood.*
Obsidian *If you hold this to the light you can see through it, as it is a type of natural glass.*
Black onxz *You can differentiate between this and obsidian because you can't see through onyx.*

Creative black stones suggest you may be wasting a lot of very vital personal power, possibly by holding onto a situation or relationship that is redundant, or by suppressing negative and probably very justifiable feelings.

Receptive Black

Buy one of these:
Dark banded agate.
Blackish grey smoky quartz.
Or look for a matt black pebble, such as flint.

Receptive black says you are feeling overwhelmed by the troubles and demands of the world, particularly those nearest to you. Now is the time to draw limits.

Red

RED is the colour of physical energy and action, putting into practice all those lovely white energies in a tangible way. It is the colour of courage and aggression. If you are buying only one to start with, choose a creative stone as this is the key stone.

Creative Red

Buy one of these:
Garnet *A sparkling rich red stone.*
Carnelian *A form of chalcedony, usually a glowing, rich cherry red.*
Red jasper *Cheap and easily obtainable. It has an opaque, vibrant gleam.*
Rhodochrosite *A dark red stone.*
Red agate *or* blood agate *Resembles a carnelian, especially when highly polished.*

Creative red suggests that you know in your heart it is time to go into battle. Sometimes you have to take your courage in both hands and fight for what you know is important.

Receptive Red

Buy one of these:
Red calcite *Pale red and looks like a piece of ice or a lozenge.*
Red fluorite *Similar to calcite, but more glassy.*
Red banded agate *Opaque with more muted reddish-brown and pink colouring than the blood agate.*
Or find for free:
A matt brick or dark red pebble *Usually sandstone or shale.*

Receptive Red suggests that you are turning your anger inwards and unfairly blaming yourself for the situation. Stop biting the heads off cream buns and turn your anger on the cause.

Orange

ORANGE is the colour of independence, one often associated with the happiness and sense of uniqueness that gives us the confidence to assert who we are and what we believe, in spite of opposition from those around. If you are only buying one orange stone choose the creative orange as this is the key crystal for this colour.

Creative Orange

Buy one of the following:
Amber *Fossilised tree resin, usually about 50 million years old, which has a rich vibrant colour*
Rich orange carnelian
Orange jasper
Orange citrine

Creative orange crystals tend to appear in a reading when you start to be aware that you don't have the same goals as those around you. Now is the time to work out what *would* make you happy and then see how this can be achieved without anger or bitterness.

Receptive Orange

But one of these:
Orange calcite
Orange shade of smoky-quartz
Agate banded with muted orange
Orange beryl
Or for free you can find:
A matt orange stone *Usually sandstone or quartzite that may have orange glints depending on what other minerals are present*

Receptive orange usually appears in a reading when we feel that our identity has somehow disappeared. So it is important to start in small ways to make time for yourself and to start to exercise your preferences.

Yellow
YELLOW is the colour of the sun and communication. It cuts through double-speak and jargon to the real issue and shatters illusion. If you are only buying one crystal in this colour choose creative yellow as this is the key stone.

Creative yellow

Buy one of these:
Yellow citrine
Topaz
Yellow zircon

Rich opaque yellow jasper
Golden-yellow tiger's eye *A beautiful lustre and rich striped markings.*
Golden amber

Creative yellow suggests that clear communication is needed to get things moving. State your opinion in a way that allows for no misunderstandings or mis-interpretation either of your views or the seriousness of your intentions.

Receptive yellow

Buy one of these:
Soft golden beryl
Yellow calcite
Yellow fluorite
Yellowy rutilated quartz *Clouded inside with yellow streaks.*
Or find for free:
A matt yellow pebble, limestone, sand-stone or shale.

Receptive Yellow suggests that you may be confused in your own mind as to what it is you really want, or you feel over-whelmed by the seeming expertise of others. Make sure you are responding to today's message, not the rejections of yesterday.

Green
GREEN crystals are the stones of our heart and when we choose them it is our heart not our head speaking. So we are very aware of our own feelings about a situation and should be guided by them. If you are buying only one green crystal,

choose a receptive green stone because this is the key crystal.

Creative green

Buy one of these:

A brilliant emerald green opaque malachite *Sometimes with black stripes or pale green streak, like a humbug.*

Deep green bloodstone flecked with red *A form of chalcedony.*

Aventurine *Deep rich green with an opaque sheen.*

Sparkling green topaz.

Green zircon *Good substitute for the more expensive emerald.*

Dark green spinel.

Yellowy-green peridot *The dazzling sister of the more muted serpentine.*

Creative green in a reading suggests that you do feel strongly about a situation, and should trust your own feelings rather than what others tell you, or maybe seems logical. Start at the heart of the matter and you won't go far wrong.

Receptive Green

Buy one of these:

Apple green chrysoprase *Another form of chalcedony.*

Soft jade *In many shades of green.*

Greeny-blue and white-flecked amazonite.

Olive green serpentine.

Transparent green fluorite *May vary from light green through to almost bottle green.*

Water-ice green calcite.

Moss agate *Really colourless but contains a profusion of tree-like growths of muted green minerals.*

Receptive green means you shouldn't accept the situation at face value, but be aware of what people are feeling deep down. Be sensitive to underlying currents and keep the self-esteem of others intact while getting what you want.

Blue

BLUE is the colour of the mind and conscious knowledge and wisdom. So when blue stones appear it is an occasion to use logic and A to B conventional thinking rather than intuitive leaps. High ideals are central to whatever issue is involved. If you are buying only one stone at first buy the creative stone as this is the key one.

Creative Blue

Buy one of these:

Howzite *A sky blue opaque stone.*

Turquoise

Rich blue azurite *sometimes flecked with paler blue.*

Lapis lazuli *or* lazurite *A deep blue flecked with gold.*

Falcon's eye *A blue version of the tiger's eye.*

Laboradite *With a brilliant bluey-green iridescence.*

Creative blue stones appear when you've got to make a decision that involves more than material issues. It's no good letting your heart rule your head. You've got to read the small print and calculate the cost not only in financial terms. It's definitely a case of sticking to conventional wisdom and looking before you leap.

Receptive Blue

Buy one of these:
Pale blue lace agate.
Dyed pale blue quartz.
Blue fluorite *Looks like a piece of smooth blue glass.*
Aquamarine *A form of beryl, varying between light and dark blue.*
Celestite *With celestial blue tints.*
Moonstone *With a bluey sheen.*

Receptive blue shows that you still can't let your feelings take over. But in this case it's a question of compromise rather than sticking to rigid principles.

Purple

VIOLET, INDIGO or PURPLE stones deal with our unconscious wisdom, intuitions and inspirations. This elusive but vital part of our being links us with our spiritual and psychic self. It is the colour of our inner magical powers that can ease and illuminate our everyday world if we just trust this hidden source. If you are only buying one stone at first choose the receptive purple stone as this is the key one.

Creative purple stones.

Buy one of these:
Opaque, densely coloured sodalite *In many shades of purple — deep indigo with white being the most common.*
Sugilite *More expensive but a beautiful bright purple.*
Iridiscent peacock ore (bornite)
Purple-shaded lapis lazuli

Creative purple stones suggest that you are questioning the meaning and purpose of your life and are seeking fulfilment in a spiritual or very creative way. You shouldn't let people laugh or belittle any life changes you are making.

Receptive purple.

Buy one of these:
Soft transparent amethyst *Which can vary from quite dark to almost colourless.*
Purple fluorite *Looks like coloured glass.*
Lilac version of kunzite.

Receptive purple stones are the stones of intuition, of seeing round corners. They tell you that this is a time to trust your hunches and go for the answer that may go against all you've been taught or told, but which you know is the way forward.

Pink
PINK represents the reconciliation of opposites or extremes and also of healing. Women are natural healers and being a woman you know that, whether there's internal or external strife, you'll be the one who has to heal the breach. If you are buying only one pink stone, choose a receptive pink as this is the key stone.

Creative pink

Buy one of these:
Pink coral
Deep pink rhodonite *Sometimes streaked with black.*
Bright to salmon pink rhodochrosite *Often banded with paler pink.*

Sugilite *Bright pink and more expensive but worth buying.*
Pink sodalite.

Creative pink stones often appear when a conflict is external and directly involves you even if it wasn't your fault. Somebody's got to break the deadlock so maybe now's a good time to make overtures.

Receptive pink

Buy on of these:
Delicately transparent rose quartz
Translucent pink mother of pearl
Soft pink watermelon tourmaline
Pink kunzite *The woman's stone*
Very pale pink calcite
Pink fluorite

Or you can get free receptive pink stones from the beach, hillside or even local recreation ground — pink and white flecked granite or matt pink sandstone pebbles.

Receptive pink crystals in a reading suggest the disharmony is within you. It's a signal to slow down and, wherever possible, avoid people and situations that cause you stress.

Brown

BROWN is the colour of the earth, so when you choose a brown crystal, it's telling you to go back to grass roots, touch home base and trust the evidence of your eyes, ears and other senses rather than rely on what others tell you. If you are buying only one brown stone initially choose the receptive version as this is the key stone.

Creative brown

But one of these:
Rich gleaming brown tiger's eye
Lustrous brown chrysoberyl
Rich brown amber
Strongly-coloured brown or yellowy-brown jasper
Rich brown or tawny single-coloured agate *The more muted stones with several bands of pale brown that merge into one another are useful as the receptive version.*

Creative brown stones show it's a nitty-gritty issue that's at the root of the problem. You'll need to take practical steps to resolve it and get things moving. Commonsense and hard graft may not move mountains, but at least can dig you a path.

Receptive brown

Buy one of these:
Petrified wood stone *In various shades of brown that you can either buy polished or find for free on beaches where there were once forests.*
Smoky-brown quartz.
Rutilated quartz *Clear quartz with golden-brown rutiles inside.*
Or you can find brown-stained limestones, perhaps containing fossils, or brown sandstone or a brown flint.

Receptive brown stones suggest you may be feeling overwhelmed by the sheer logistics of your life and exhausted from juggling the practical demands of work and home commitments. You're probably doing more than your share of the hard slog. Get every one else moving while you delegate.